Gwen —

Hope Possible

To HOPE!

Doryn Kagan

Hope Possible

A Network News Anchor's Thoughts On Losing Her Job, Finding
Love, A New Career, and My Dog, Always My Dog

DARYN KAGAN

Tree Swan Publishing

ISBN: 0578173921
ISBN 13: 9780578173924

To My Mr. SummerFest
And funnel cakes.
Thank goodness for funnel cakes.

"The Big Reveal before the wedding. Atlanta, Georgia. September 2012." Book cover and this photo credit: Bliss Photography

Contents

Hey, There

You.

Yeah, you.

If the idea of this book appealed to you enough to pick it up or download, I'm betting you might've had some kind of loss.

A job.

A great love.

Better health.

Or maybe you're just so, so tired of waiting for those wonderful things to show up.

I get it.

In 2010, the wonderful folks at The Dayton Daily News gave me a fine challenge: create a newspaper column that talks about overcoming obstacles.

Me, who was told after 12 years at CNN that the network would not be renewing my contract.

Me, who always wanted to get married and have kids and found myself still single well into my 40's.

Being 40-something with no job prospects, no husband, and no kids was hardly my grand life plan realized.

"The more you share of your own personal story, the better," my wise editor, Jana Collier, encouraged.

Of course, going "there" went against everything I was taught as a traditional journalist. But sweet, patient, Jana pushed. "Tell a story, that's a article," she explained. "Share your story and challenges, that's a column."

The layers have come off more and more as "What's Possible" has grown into a nationally syndicated column. Meanwhile, friends and family have become shocked and concerned about how much of my messy life I've chosen to share.

Hey, "Call, Jana!" I tell them. "I'm just doing my job."

As I spill my mess onto these pages, I just want to thank you for sharing some of your mess with mine.

I'm honored.

If my words give you just a glimmer that you're not alone, that things really can get better, not perfect, but better, well, then, our time together will be well spent.

A reinvention of what is now possible.

One note, I've chosen not to share these columns in chronological order. This book isn't so much a timeline, as it a collection of thoughts.

Call it, "artsy."

Call me, "lazy."

I see it as a nod to accepting that life is messy and the good stuff doesn't have to show up in order. Mine certainly hasn't.

To our messes, to what's possible---

Single Days

I didn't wait for marriage.

Judge me if you want for not holding out. I will simply point the finger at an old boyfriend. Oh, and my mother.

The Gift

First, my mother, who on the occasion of my 40th birthday, sat across from me with my grandmother's beautiful antique silver tea set on a tray between us.

"I had always planned on giving this to you when you got married," she sighed. "But, well…"

Yes, it was understood that with my having not been engaged before my 40th birthday and with no prospects on the horizon, it would be silly to wait for something that clearly, disappointingly, was never going to happen.

The Jerk

Then, there was the old boyfriend who got great joy out of sharing how joyous his upcoming wedding was going to be.

We interrupt this column for you to pass judgment again on me. "Daryn, what were your doing talking to an old boyfriend who was going to marry someone else?"

Hey, we worked together. He made it hard to avoid him in the hallway.

"Daryn, what were you thinking dating someone you worked with? You know those things never end well!"

Hey, the newspaper didn't give me this column because I've led a perfect life. Rather, because I'm not afraid to be honest about my messy one.

Back to creepy, narcissistic ex-boyfriend who loved describing his pre-wedding festivities. "The best part was my old friends meeting my current friends," he shared.

Hello, extra cruel twist of the knife through my heart.

See, I was never the girl who dreamed of the big princess dress or the first dance. No, for me, my wedding was going to be that awesome moment when my people would meet my people. Well, and cake, too. I did fantasize a lot about the cake. But really, a wedding is the time you get to share this incredible collection of people you've met up until that point of your life.

Jerked Into Action

That conversation tipped me into action.

If I didn't have to be married to get Nana's tea set, why did I have to wait for my people to meet my people?

And so, I decided to throw my own party.

What would it be?

That's where the fun part comes in.

It's My Party

When you're planning an event that has no name, no tradition, no significant other to consult, you can create whatever the heck you want.

For me, that became, "Soul Spa."

I invited my best girlfriends to gather for a long weekend focusing on being happy and creating our dreams. They might've thought I was nuts, but they all came, from my best friend in kindergarten to my CNN producer who went to cover the war with me for CNN.

We bonded, shared dreams, got massages, and built a big bon fire to burn ideas and relationships that no longer served us.

Oh, and you can bet there was cake.

A lot of cake.

Amazingly, or maybe not, some incredible things happened over next few years. Two friends who had been struggling with infertility got pregnant. Another got the job she'd been working towards. A few found love.

My own manifesting was much slower. It wasn't until six years after "Soul Spa" that I met the man who would become my husband.

My People Meet My People—Again

When we did decide to marry two years later, just about every Soul Spa-ster traveled from around the country to be there. I think they were happy to share in our happiness. They also wanted to see the women they bonded with eight years before. My people had become their people.

I share my story, Dear Reader, to ask, "What are you waiting for? What private joy have you been putting off?"

It's time to stop waiting.

Don't wait for the wedding, the baby shower, those extra 20 pounds to come off.

It's time to throw a party.

Now.

A party with no rules.

And, for those who suggest you're nuts, just blame it my long ago ex-boyfriend, We're showing you, pushing you, to see, the time to create your joy is now.

I'm hoping that's an invitation that just might be impossible to turn down.

Other Side of The Single Fence

"It sure would be nice," my friend sighed as we caught up on each other's lives.

She was particularly taken with the addition of my beau, Mr. SummerFest, who I met just over a year ago.

I understand that sigh more than most. It's the "How Do I Possibly Get Over That Side of The Single Fence?" sigh.

It's possible many people are hoping, wanting and trying to get over to the coupled side, as if being single is some sort of obstacle to overcome. As if, once you're "over there," you're set for life.

As someone who has never married and has spent some good chunks of my adult life uncoupled, I get it. I'm one of those who has read the New York Times "Vows" section each Sunday. I've been in complete awe over the seemingly simple act of a woman finding a man who loves her and wants to commit to a life with her. It has felt as foreign to me as I imagine my TV news and media career has felt to most folks.

Now that I am on that other side of the single fence, now that I do have the great guy who wants to commit and make that life, I feel the need to reach back to those still single and assure them that single is not an obstacle to overcome.

Yes, I love having someone wonderful to share my life with. I just can't take credit for getting from here to there. It's not like I lost 100 pounds, finally joined an online dating site or became a blonde. We were casually introduced by mutual friends when we ran into each other at a summer festival. Hence his nickname, Mr. SummerFest.

I can also see that standing on this side of the coupled fence is not necessarily a permanent place. We'd like to think that once you've found The One, you're set for life. I know my friend who lost her husband to cancer last month would tell me differently.

Then, there are the two friends going divorces right now. They each had those golden couple kind of marriages that made me feel like for years that I was missing out. Turns out, one husband was a long-time cheat. My other friend recently confessed that she'd actually been miserable and lonely for years as she and her husband led separate lives.

I'll enjoy this side of the coupled fence, appreciating that it might not last forever.

Before I met Mr. SummerFest, I had made three lists. One described the man I thought I wanted to meet. One described what we would be like as a couple. The third listed who I would be and what I would be like as my highest self if I were in that dream relationship.

It recently occurred to me that I'm so happy with Mr. SummerFest because I like who I am with him. A funny thing happens when you realize that. The other lists just aren't as important. It becomes pretty easy to let go the idea of the package you thought he was going to show up in.

The punch line is I didn't have to wait for the guy to show up. The one thing I could control—who I am, how I show up in life, I got to start doing right away.

Turns out the obstacle to overcome, the fence to jump over wasn't finding the other person.

It was finding my best self.

Got Kids?

"Wanted to know if you had any children?"

The question came in a short follow up email from a producer trying to book me for an interview.

What an appropriate question, I thought, as we find ourselves in the Mother's Day season.

So, here are the short answers:

Have I birthed children: No.

Do I have children: Yes.

I'm actually overflowing in the kid department. By last count, there are 10 godchildren, two nephews and two special girls who get large chunks of my time, attention, love and devotion.

Perhaps, you're like me. The picture you had for motherhood didn't pan out like you planned. Like most women, I always thought I would be a mom in the traditional sense. But when I found myself at what felt like the "now or never moment," having a baby or adopting would've meant intentionally becoming a single mother.

"Do the baby now," some friends encouraged. "The guy can always come along later." With all due respect to women who have made that choice, it didn't seem right for me.

I've always celebrated and surrounded myself with kids, so loved ones were concerned when I told them I'd decided not to have my own.

And then, a funny thing happened when I closed the door on having my own baby—my life filled up with kids.

I've shared how close I am with my beau's 12-year-old daughter. He's been a single dad since her mom died a few years ago, so there's plenty of room for me.

Even before I met them, I made one of the best decisions of my life. I became a Big Sister in the Big Brother Big Sister program. In 2009, I was matched with then 8-year-old Rodneisha. Our backgrounds, skin color, and ages couldn't be more different. Yet, from the first moment I met Ro, it was like meeting a little me. A girl who loves to read, learn new things, play word games, and have adventures.

We do little things like bake cookies. And big things like take trips. She bet me she could get straight A's in 4th grade, a sucker bet if there ever was one. The payoff? I took her to San Francisco last year. It was her first time on an airplane. As we stepped into the airport, her arm went out pointing to something a few feet away. "Wow! Look at that!" she exclaimed. "Sweetie," I smiled. "That's where the suitcases come out when you arrive," I said as I explained the luggage carousel.

Before we took off she also started educating me. "Daryn," she said. "You told me this was an airport."

"Uh, yes," I replied.

"But it's also a train station, a shopping mall and an art gallery!" she delighted.

Indeed she's right, as we had to take an underground train to get to the plane, saw sculptures along the way, and buzzed past a zillion shops—all things that had just been a blur to me before.

Then, there are moments like Rodneisha getting ready to jump off a diving board for the first time last summer.

"Daryn, do you think I can do it?" she asked me.

I still tear up thinking of the honor and enormity of this special girl looking to me to define what's possible in her young life.

These days, life revolves around the schedules of these special kids in my life rather than breaking news and climbing the corporate network news ladder.

As my friends like to say, "For someone who doesn't have kids, you sure do have a lot of kids!"

In this Mother's Day season, let me salute all you moms out there, including my own, who is turning 75 this year.

For anyone who is feeling the loss of kids in your life, I'm happy to share my journey. I found it's not that I was meant to have kids.

Kids were meant to have me.

I can't quite do it yet.

I need some space.

Before I'm ready.

It's like that with great loves.

This one has been with me for years.

I suspect with you, as well.

A love that can only be found between the pages

Of books.

Reading.

Diving into the deep end with characters I like and relate to better than some of the "real" people in my life.

My name is Daryn and I'm a life-long book lover.

You, too, Dear Reader? Are you a fellow Reader?

And if so, what kind?

Book love is sort of like dating.

How we look for it, enjoy it, pace it.

Are you a serial reader? The kind who jumps from book to book? Your soul starts to shake if you're not involved in some master plot?

Do you refuse any exclusive relationship, reading more than one book at once?

Me?

I'm a one-book-at-a-time kinda gal.

And I need a little space between tomes.

After all, reading a book is so gosh darn intimate. For days, weeks, months, these characters and I grab every spare moment together. I will read in bed, in the bathroom while blow drying my hair (and you thought I didn't have talent!)

And if the book is really good, like the one I just finished, I fall in love.

This is not the wisest of choices as I know how this is going to end.

Just as all unrequited love does—

Not well.

For, to love a book is to give your heart away, to the characters, to their struggles.

Meanwhile, they don't know who I am.

The idea that they're now sharing their story with the next book-aholic eager to gobble up their pages hurts my warped feelings a bit, I must say.

That's why, like dating, I can't jump immediately from one book to another.

So, yes, that makes this a lonely time, as I'm currently between books.

I crawl into bed thinking of that book I forgot that I finished, only to remember, "Oh, that's right. We're not together anymore."

My heart pangs, just not enough to move along.

Not quite yet.

Sometime over the next week or two, I'll start thinking about dipping my page turning finger.

Like someone ready to get back in the dating pool, I'll casually ask friends, "Know any good books?"

Or maybe I'll look for an online match asking on Twitter and Facebook, "What book have you loved lately?"

A good fix-up requires some information, so let me just say, I don't have a certain type. I bounce from what the book world likes to call, "Women's Fiction," to thrillers, and if I'm feeling kinda smart, some literary stuff.

I've been known to spend my fair share of time with the likes of John Grisham, Dan Silva, Lisa Scottoline, Kristin Harmel, Harlan Coben, Ken Follett, and most recently Liane Moriarty.

How about you?

Who you reading?

How you reading?

I've got time to talk before the next book steals my time and heart.

Note To Self I Wish I'd Had All Those Years

"Dear 20, 30, & 40 yr-old Self:

It's possible you're obsessing about all the guys who dumped you, broke your heart, who you were so convinced were "The One?"

Yeah, I know, there have been some, "Will Someone Ever Really Love Me?" ugly cry moments.

I want you to know if you just hang in there, you're going to meet this guy who was put on this earth to be an awesome husband and father.

Yeah, there are such guys.

No joke.

He might not be the CEO of some big corporation, the best athlete, or drive the fanciest car. But, he will be the strongest and most masculine kind of man—the kind that puts his family above all else.

Don't freak out or anything, but this is the kind of guy who will pick you to be his wife.

I know, sounds crazy, right?

July 2014 will be your second wedding anniversary and that same guy is going to send you gorgeous flowers with a mushy note attached claiming to be the luckiest guy in the world.

I know this is all so hard to believe from where you're sitting, plopped on your bedroom floor surrounded by with soggy Kleenex and a half-eaten pint of Haagen-Dazs.

Actually, who are we kidding?

We both know you ate the whole pint.

You're kind of a pathetic sight right now, but I want you to know there is hope.

Don't get me wrong.

It's going to take some work.

You'll need the help of some awesome, loving friends. Those self-help books you keep devouring that don't seem to be doing any good are actually seeping some wisdom into the stubborn brain of yours.

Some sessions with a good therapist will also help unravel that spaghetti that is your brain and Man Picker.

Defeated Self, when you least expect it, when you completely give up, you're going to start looking at the good guys differently.

Oh, it'll seem a little weird at first, but you'll figure out a way to get used to a man who is crazy about you, who would never dream that you should settle for a few crumbs of himself that he tosses your way.

No, he'll offer up the entire cookie. Shoot, forget the cookie—this husband would go to the ends of the earth to deliver the entire bakery!

So, hang in there.

Dreams do come true.

I promise.

In the meantime, Big Hugs!

Love, Me.

Love And Marriage

Don't Judge The Packaging

"Daddy tricked me!" my 12-year-old friend recounted as she remembered last Christmas.

The girl I now call my "Sweet Sprout" shared how she wanted an Apple iTouch more than anything she could remember. But as the stack of presents under the tree dwindled to just one she had to give up hope. The one remaining gift featured a large size box. No way did it resemble the kind of package she knew an iTouch would come in.

"As I started to unwrap and unwrap," she said as her crystal blue eyes began to twinkle, "I started to think, 'Maybe, just maybe...'"

Sure enough, as Sprout made it through the layers of tissue...there it was —the iTouch! Her ticket to texting, listening to music and playing games. It was rarely been out of her hands since. Well, except for the time it got thrown in with the laundry. But that's a story for another day.

Today is about something that took me much longer than Sprout's 12-years to learn. Sometimes, the best presents come to us by total surprise, in packages we could've never guessed.

By this time last year, I had pretty much given up on the gift I've wanted more than anything for the longest time.

A family.

I have been blessed a million times over in my life. With good health, good friends, an amazing career, even great love. But the man who thinks I hung the moon, shares my values, makes me laugh, and just as importantly wants to make a life with me. The guy who wants to dream big and find joy in what can be the drudgery of everyday life?

That big Mac Daddy gift of gifts has been elusive.

And so, 2010 was the year I gave in. Accepted my fate that I would live and love all the opportunities a single life brings. I decided to be happy with what I had. All well and good. Still, I'd be lying if I didn't share that I had some pretty low moments longing for the connection that a shared life brings.

It was on such a sad day that I agreed to go to an early summer festival with two of my best friends, a gay couple, Craig and Michael. They are just the kind of friends every single gal feels comfortable with, yet, let's be honest, hardly who you would expect to be the source of finding good dating material. In general, that might be true, except that Craig and Michael are also parents to an 11-year-old boy. My godson, Cooper.

As I yet again played fourth-wheel to their sweet family and strolled through booths of arts and crafts that no one seems to buy, Craig spotted a fellow Dad from their son's elementary school standing in the line to buy Funnel Cakes.

"Why don't you and your daughter come sit down with us and have lunch?" he offered simply thinking "the more the merrier."

As they approached, the other dad, Michael instantly thought of a whole different agenda. "Single! Single! Single! Incoming!" he announced while slugging my arm. I could've about died from embarrassment and to this day give thanks for the loud band that was playing.

It was a brief meeting that day with the man who has come to be known amongst my people as, "Mr. SummerFest." I learned he was a single dad dedicated to raising his 11-year-old daughter ever since his ex-wife passed away a few years ago. It was enough for me to go, "hmmmm," and for Michael to reach out through the school's parent contact sheet to see if Mr. SummerFest might be interested.

Two gay boyfriends and funnel cakes.

There's a formula no one has ever offered in one of those "How To Find a Great Guy" books.

I can see now that Christmas came for me this year in June. Mr. SummerFest is that man. "Fully-assembled," one of my other friends declared after meeting him. A grown up who's been knocked down by life, gotten back up and not wasted the opportunities to grow. The fact that we share values, like to play, and he's pretty darn good-looking are the bows on top of that gift I didn't see coming.

As the holidays approached, we got late word that a variety of our people would be in town. "Let's make a party," I declared at the last minute.

Somehow, Mr. SummerFest is delighted by one of my biggest joys—my people meeting my people. In 12 hours, I whipped together a buffet.

There we all were gathered in my living room—Mr. SummerFest, his daughter, "Sprout," his late ex-wife's parents, and the family of my mother's best childhood friend who just happen to be passing through town on Christmas Eve.

The makings for an episode of "Modern Family," if ever there was one.

As I looked around the living room at this eclectic bunch, I had to smile. There it was --the present and the packaging I could've never imagined.

A family.

I share my holiday, thinking that you just might be taking inventory of the gifts you received this year. Perhaps, you're also making a list of the gifts you're hoping might show up in the New Year.

May I suggest you be ready.

If you're willing to let go any pre-conceived notion of who might deliver the gift and the packaging it shows up in, Christmas just might be on its way.

The Spoon That Held Hope I'd One Day Find Love

It must've been about four years ago when I first heard about The Spoon.

Some of my best lady friends and I were on a Girls' Trip to Charleston, SC. You know the kind where you leave behind the stresses of everyday life and head off to relax, eat too much, and laugh and explore.

We ladies were taking a historic tour of downtown Charleston, South Carolina where the guide did an awesome job describing not only architecture and history, but also the longtime local customs of the area that was once dominated by rice plantations.

"A lady was not considered a proper Southern Bride," Wonderful Guide Lady explained, "until she'd been gifted with a Charleston Rice Spoon."

She happened to have one handy as she explained it might look like a regular silver serving spoon with a long handle, "Now look at the other end," she instructed. "The bowl is bigger. It's the size of a human hand and it always dishes up a perfect serving of rice."

I was fascinated with the idea of this spoon, as I have been most things connected to marriage and weddings.

See, I've done some really big things in my life: been a network news anchor, traveled the world, loved, been loved. But the idea that a man I loved would want to marry me and make a life together—that seemed as far away and out of reach as some of my adventures might seem to you.

Just as I had pretty much given up on that dream about two years ago, along comes the man I like to refer to in this column as "Mr. SummerFest." We were introduced by mutual friends at a summer festival weeks before he happened to be moving a couple blocks down from me in my same neighborhood. Not quite the boy-next-door, but boy-next-block sure was nice after too many long distance relationships.

We've had a wonderful two years of love, friendship, and a lot of fun. Two weeks ago, Mr. SummerFest lured my dog, my three-legged cat and then me, into my backyard in front of my three chickens.

It was there he got down on one knee and asked me to be his wife. There was no flash mob, nothing you will see with a million hits on YouTube.

"There was no place on Earth I could think of," he explained, "That would mean more to you than in front of all your animals."

He was right.

It was perfect.

Oh, to be known and be loved.

And so, that brings me to last Saturday. My friend, Tricia, and I wrapped up our weekly ladies run. "I have something for you," she said.

There sitting amidst a bridey gift bag and lots of tissue paper was, you might've guessed, my very own Charleston Rice Spoon.

Turns out she's had it for me since that trip four years ago.

I can't stop looking at that spoon and smiling.

Smiling for seemingly impossible dreams that do come true.

Smiling for friends that hold space and believe in my wishes long before I dare to.

And of course, smiling for the always perfect servings of rice I will dish up in the home I will soon share with my Mr. SummerFest.

The truth is I've been holding out on you.

I did indeed share last summer how my then boyfriend got down on his knee in front of my dog, my three-legged cat and three chickens and proposed. It was a wonderful moment.

Truth is, it's only half the story of what happened that day.

Several hours later, after calling family and friends, and going out to celebrate, I found myself in my bedroom with the 13-year-old daughter of my freshly-minted fiance.

"Are you really happy?" she wanted to know.

"I really am," I shared, knowing there was one more question that needed to be asked. "Daddy asked me to marry him and now I have a proposal for you."

She looked back at me with wonder.

"Once Daddy and I are married, if it's okay with you, I'd like to adopt you," I offered in a somewhat shaky emotional voice.

Her beautiful blue eyes got really big and she asked, "What would that mean?"

Smart kid. Read the fine print before signing up for a life-changing event. She certainly has seen plenty change in her young life. Saw her parents divorce. Saw her mom pass away when she was only 8-years-old. Saw her father do the best he could raising a young girl alone.

"Good question!" I assured her. We talked about all the families we know who have adopted children. She has one cousin from China. Another one is on the way from Ethiopia. There's her friend, Claire, who was adopted at birth. Her friend, Genevieve, was raised by her single mom until her mom got married a few years ago and her new stepdad became her legal dad. And there's Cooper, the son of Craig and Michael, the couple who introduced me to my new family.

"This isn't about replacing your mom," I assured her. "The way I see it, your mom did something I couldn't. She gave birth to you. Could you imagine if I had done that? You would have all my genes!"

The thought brought on the half-laugh half horrified look I expected, having been told plenty of times in the last year, "You're so weird!"

"Your mom started the job of raising you," I kept on. "I know if I had started that amazing job and had to leave too soon, my biggest wish from heaven would be that someone would come along and love you and raise like you were her own. That's how I feel and that's what I want to do."

There was a pause, that for me felt like an hour, when in reality it was probably only a few seconds. "You'd really want to adopt me?" she asked, not believing.

"I do," I told her. "As much as I want to marry Daddy, but only if and when you want it. We can do it soon, next year, or never. It's totally up to you."

I've always let her control the speed our relationship. "You don't get to choose who your father dates," I told her during our first heart to heart talk two years ago, "but you will always get to decide how much you and I do together. You steer that ship."

She jumped into my arms. "I really want you to adopt me!" she exclaimed.

Talk about a big day!

I share the rest of the proposal story now, because five months after I married her dad, the documents have been gathered and the papers filed. We go before a judge this week. I am excited for this day as I was for my wedding.

I know I started to love her the day I met her and her dad. If all goes well, by the time you read this column I will be able to call her legally what she has already been in my heart for a long time.

My daughter.

"Among the many benefits of opening my heart to
my Lucky Charm—getting an up-do."

As lucky charms go, mine is not shy.

"Daryn, you should write a column about me," she strongly suggested this week.

Since she is the one who, I believe, changed my life for the best ever, hers is a request I'm sure to fulfill.

So, here goes.

She showed up at one of those low times.

One of those, "Feel sorry for myself, this is never going to get better, I'm on verge of getting bitter, Pity Party for One," kind of low times.

Dear Reader, you've had one or six of those times yourself, yes?

For me, it was about being well into my 40's. No marriage. No kids. Just plenty of lonely.

For my life long best friend, it was about doing the best thing possible. Turning off the spigot of listening, compassion, and understanding.

Enough.

"I think you'd like this," the email said, aong with a link to the Big Brothers Big Sisters organization.

Volunteer? Give a few hours a month of my precious time to take on someone else's drama and challenges?

"What do I need that for?" I asked full of doubt.

"Because you do," Best Friend replied.

No world famous doctor has ever written a better prescription.

I met my Lucky Charm when she was 8-years-old. An adorable package of ponytails and knowing brown eyes that devoured every book she could get her hands on.

We started slow.

Baking cookies led to movies, which led to sleepovers. Which led to jumping off the high dive at the pool. Which led to her first plane ride.

"What is the best part of having a Big Sister?" a form question asked during our second year together.

Would it be the cookies? The movies? The trips?

"She makes me feel safe," she wrote in her 9-year-old printing.

It took this kid, this tiny package of energy, to show me my life could be so much more than a lonely Sunday night.

Someone opens and explodes your heart like that there's no going back. Lucky Charm stretched my heart to make room for the dreams I thought I had, but really hadn't been ready for.

Exactly one year after the day I met my Lucky Charm, I met the man who is now my husband and the girl who is now my daughter.

Accident?

I can't see how.

Somehow, the four of us have melded into this Modern Family. No one looks alike. We have three different last names.

Five years later, Lucky Charm is now a teenager which means, uh, yeah, I'm not quite sure who we're going to get every other weekend when we have her.

"Funny, quirky, still looking at the world in an amazing way" Girl. Or "Moody nothing I do is right, but I had better not ever give a single thought about leaving her side" Girl.

The days of cookies and simple sleepovers seem long ago and so innocent.

These days, we spend endless hours applying to private high schools and scholarships for next year. Because no kid deserves to go to a school with a 40% graduation rate.

Certainly, not my Lucky Charm.

Now, what gets me down is that it's acceptable for a brilliant kid to go to a school where it's just understood 60% of the students will drop out.

So, we fill out forms, and wait. Who will give Lucky Charm her big opportunity? This kid is going places.

"She's so lucky to have you," people tell me when they see us together.

"She's lucky, alright," I agree. "She's my lucky. My Lucky Charm. She changed my world for the best. It's all I can do to help change hers."

I share my Lucky Charm with you today, well, because she asked.

And maybe, just maybe, you're in the middle of your own ongoing pity party.

The answer, I promise you, is not in your wallowing.

It's in your lucky charm. She's out there.

As my best friend was once brave enough to say to me, "Enough."

Go find a place to open your heart.

I think you're really going to like this.

How I Found A Husband: I Settled

"Help!" the email started. "I need some words of encouragement for my 43-year-old never been married friend!"

Of all the pleas this forever-single columnist thought she would never get–that probably has to be it. When you don't get married for the first time until you're 49, you hardly think you'll be the one to be giving out advice on how to find a husband.

Yet, as I close in on my first wedding anniversary, I look back thinking there is something I did that helped me find a fine man.

The simple truth is, I settled.

Whoa! Hold on. I know those are the two words anxious single women around the world dread to hear.

Nails on a chalkboard.

Please, hear me out.

My journey to finding my husband started with making a three-part list.

List One was all the things I was hoping to find in my dream man. I tossed out criticism like, "You're too picky." Height, weight, what he does for a living. One blue eye, one green eye. I went to town. The more specific, the better.

I'd heard of doing such a list before in magazines and talk shows. "Dream Up Your Dream Man!" However, I think it was the other two lists that really made the difference.

List Two was "What Will My Guy And I Look Like As A Couple?" This is where I pictured things like how much time would we spend together, how would we support each other? What would we do for fun? Again, the more specific the vision, the better.

And then came List Three: "What Will I Look Like As My Best Self When I'm In This Loving And Supportive Relationship?"

That's where the magic happened. Who did I want to be in the world? How did I want to give? How was I going to make myself happy?

As I worked on that third list, I realized I didn't have to wait for the guy to become her. I could start right away.

That's what I mean by "I settled."

I finally settled into the woman I wanted to be.

The three lists took the sting out of what could be considered bad dates.

And by "bad," I mean these are so bizarre I could write a Chick Lit novel, but no would ever believe such weird things happen.

These were no longer tragic, disappointing events, just simply information that the guy didn't match my lists.

I chose to believe that The Three List Guy was on his way.

And now, as I look over at my husband snoozing in bed as I write this early in the morning on my laptop, I'm reminded why he's such a gift.

More than any man I've ever known, he loves and supports my best version of me, the woman I envisioned on List Three. It's who he sees even on the days I'm not her, which, let me assure you are plenty!

I passed along my journey of The Three Lists to my friend, and now to you, realizing that it was important to do all three lists, and for far too long I'd been focused on the wrong thing.

I'd spent countless hours and angst of my single years looking for HIM. When really, the person I needed to be looking for was my best version of me.

Single gals, are you up for the challenge? Get your lists going.

You get to start today and there's a good chance it will lead you to a man different and better than you would have expected before.

It's time to settle.

A stranger took my breath away this week.

What would you do if a woman you just met told you, "I'm really not a risk taker," followed by, "I married a man who told me on our first date that he only had 18 months to live."

"How'd that work out for you?" I couldn't help but ask.

"He lived 18 more years past that first date. We were married for 15 of those," Brenda Zimmer Gibson told me. "They were the most amazing years of my entire life."

Brenda had reached out after she read my column a couple weeks ago about finding a husband. "It wasn't about finding him," I wrote. "It was about settling into the woman I wanted to be."

"You have it so right," she said. "I spent several years single finding out who I was supposed to be and when I did, he found me."

Brenda was sweet enough to share stories from her marriage to Gene. "We danced, we laughed, we traveled," she said. And along the way they fought cancer—together. "I focused on seeing him well and he chose to do the same."

That spirit bought them 15 more years than doctors told Gene he would have when he was first diagnosed in the early nineties.

He died just over a year ago. "Last year when you were marrying the love of your life, I was losing mine," Brenda wrote in that first email to me referring to my recent marriage and the loss of her husband.

To hear her talk about her beloved today, I can tell he is still very much alive in her heart. I suspect he always will be.

"What did you learn about love?" I asked her.

"It sounds cliché," Brenda replied, "but cancer was our greatest gift and teacher. It made us savor every minute and not waste time. I'm not saying that we didn't get annoyed with each other, but we got over it quickly because we didn't want to waste time."

"And what are you learning about loss?" I treaded lightly.

"That I was one of the luckiest people ever. I had for 15 years what some people don't have for 15 minutes."

"Some people might wonder if it was worth the risk, now that you're alone," I said.

"I wouldn't trade a day of it, even Gene's final days in the hospital," she said.

And then Brenda Gibson said something I think I will remember the rest of my life.

"The truth is, when you love someone, there never is enough time."

She did it again.

I had to catch my breath, thinking of my husband, my kids, of one of my best friends having breast cancer surgery this week. There will never be enough time with any of them.

By the time we hung up, I realized Brenda was right. She and Gene didn't take a risk. They had a safety net. A daily reminder of what is true for all of us—our time is limited.

How would you be different with your love if you remembered tomorrow wasn't promised?

I do believe Brenda Gibson just gave me a lesson in being a better wife.

She found me just in time.

This confession might shock you.

There are three little words that are really hard for me to say.

Sometimes, they even get stuck in my throat.

Me, who writes each week about love, who shares how happy I am in my new marriage, how much I love being a mom.

I have a hard time saying, "I love you."

It's no big mystery to me why it's so challenging. I didn't grow up in an "I love you" kind of house. Don't get me wrong. I was clear my parents loved me in the way they took care of us kids. We were clothed, fed, and provided every opportunity. You might go so far as to say we were spoiled. I grew up feeling loved and confident.

But, I can count on one hand the number of times I've heard my mother say, "I love you." We've never talked about, "Why?" I've always figured she probably didn't grow up in an "I love you" family, either.

A few years ago, I decided this was something I wanted to change. I started with my closest friends because I have some amazing friends and wanted them to know how I felt about them.

"There's something I want to change," I said. "Instead of ending phone calls with 'Talk to you soon,' I want to say, 'I love you.'"

They loved the idea encouraging to me break out of my more closed emotional shell.

I tried "I love you" for a few weeks. Honestly, I might as well have taken off all my clothes and danced around the city naked. I felt that exposed and uncomfortable. Not surprisingly, within a few weeks I was back to ending calls with, "Talk to you soon."

Funny, how life has a way of pushing you along.

Turns out I have now married into an "I love you" kind of family. My husband of one year says it all the time. Thank goodness he's not a scorekeeper on who says it most and he doesn't need to hear it back every time he says it to me. He has the wisdom to see my love in all that I do, if not all that I say.

Then there is the ultimate "I love you" trainer, my new daughter who I adopted last Spring. The way she so naturally says, "Good night! I love you!" Or gets out of the car when I drop her off at school, "Bye! I love you!"

It's enough to make my heart explode.

It makes me realize that discomfort takes a back seat to what's important. My kid will hear that I love her.

You can believe I found a way to say those words to one of my best friends the night before her breast cancer surgery last month.

I'm hoping practice makes perfect, that if I say it enough times it'll start to feel natural.

I love you, Husband.

I love you, Daughter (even if I did say, 'No, you cannot go to the midnight premiere showing of 'City of Bones' movie with your friends on a school night.')

How about you? Do you know the feeling of feeling love, but not loving to say love? If so, I'd love to hear from you.

I promise, we can wrap our conversation with, "Talk to you later."

The Thing I Should've Known About Love

I gave a little prayer of thanks this morning as I walked my dog in the still morning dark.

Thanks that my husband made it home last night.

Was he gone on a business trip?

No.

Pushing limits on a drunken bender?

Oh, that's a funny one, if you knew him.

Was he somewhere I should've been worried about?

Not at all.

He was,

Are you ready for this?

At his first baseball game of the season.

Every Spring, he pulls out the bat, mitt, stretchy pants, high socks and baseball hat and joins his men's baseball league.

Baseball means once a week when he leaves for work I won't see him until the next morning because he gets home from these games way past my bedtime.

Have I really turned into Her?

Forever single gal, now a couple years into marriage is now Clingy Wife?

Hardly.

I love that he has a thing.

Just for him.

Pure fun.

This is just another lesson that marriage has taught me about love.

Simply, it's easier to be the one who leaves.

The one who walks out the door.

Who gets to go.

For you, too, Dear Reader?

You, who probably knew this even without marriage.

I'm just slower than most figuring this stuff out.

The more you love, the harder it is to see that love walk out the door.

Harder to be the one who watches your kid get on the school bus.

Easier to be the friend who goes on the journey, rather than the one who stays behind to worry.

"Be safe," Husband will say to me as his final words whenever I leave the house, be it to drive one of the kids across town or meet a girlfriend for coffee.

"How silly," I think to myself. I feel safe when it's my turn to be the one who leaves.

I've been around the world and back in my days as a news anchor and reporter. Never once did I worry that I was going to be okay. I do have faint recollection of my parents and friends worrying as I covered a war in the Middle East or volunteered at an orphanage in Africa.

I was fine because I could see I was fine.

I was the one who got to go. I had a faint idea that it was harder for the ones left behind.

Now, that I'm married and a mom, I know this to be true.

So, when the neighborhood owl hooted me awake this morning, first thing I did was look over to the other side of the bed.

There he was.

Husband.

Snoozing away, probably dreaming of *almost* beating the best team in the league last night.

And so I smiled as I walked DarlaDog down our street in the final moments of darkness.

He was just gone for a small thing.

And he made it home.

Safe.

When you love someone, that's no small thing.

Wedding Vows: The Most Important Thing No One Will Tell You

It's possible an absolutely brilliant, inspired wedding ceremony is happening about now, just as you and I sit down to have our weekly time together.

I actually can't tell you the name of the couple getting married.

Our paths crossed a couple of weeks ago as my family spent some time on a beach in Southern California.

Hard to miss these two gorgeous people who looked like they stepped out a picture frame you buy at a department store.

Perfect beautiful couple like you'd expect to see in Southern California.

Gorgeous, except for their furrowed brows.

"What's wrong?" I had to ask.

"We're getting married right here at this spot in a couple of weeks," the man explained.

"We're here to check out the venue," the woman chimed in, as they look concerned at the roaring surf.

"We're worried the crashing waves will be too loud to hear our vows," he explained.

"Most brilliant thing you can do," I assured them.

They looked at me like the crazy lady who talks to strangers, which of course, I am.

I explained how my husband and I got married two years ago next to a waterfall in North Carolina.

"Just like you, we scouted that location two weeks before we wed. We thought it was perfect. A mild flow cascading over some giant boulders into a peaceful pool down below where we would stand and say our vows."

"That sounds wonderful," the bride-to-be said.

"We thought it would be, too," I agreed. "Only, it rained for the next two weeks solid. When we came back with our girls and an officiant to do the wedding, that peaceful pool had grown into a lake. The simple waterfall looked like a million fire hydrants roaring on full blast."

"Hanging onto each other as we say our vows, trying not to fall into the booming, overflowing water at Silver Run Falls, North Carolina."

Photo credit: Tiffany Anne Photography

"What did you do?" the future groom asked.

"We went ahead with the wedding," I shared. "My husband and I had to hold onto each other for dear life just not to fall in, which turns out to be a good analogy for married life."

"And the vows?" the young woman asked. "Could you even hear what the other was saying?"

"Not a single word," I replied. "That's what made it perfect."

Two years into marriage, here's the thing I've figured out about wedding vows—

It's all well and good to promise all sorts of stuff, romantic, devoted, and cute.

Truth is, though, you have no idea what life is going to serve up, what surprises you're signing up for.

"When did I promise to let one of your ailing pet chickens spend the night inside the house instead in the coop where she belongs?" my husband asks.

"You don't remember that part of the waterfall vows?" I ask innocently to end the conversation.

"When did I agree to go to bed with a loud, crinkly bag of frozen peas icing down your sore shoulder?" I asked the other night.

"Waterfall vows," he said.

He had me.

And of course, that's just the small stuff. Families, schedules, quirks, stress can make this marriage thing challenging.

To the couple getting married on the beach, I say, "Let that ocean roar!"

To engaged couples, forget stressing over the dress, the cake (well, make sure there is good cake,) the bridal party. Get married somewhere loud.

Book a marching band, a wood chipper, or a jackhammer to fire away while you say your vows.

To Husband, I shout, "Thank you for the two best years of my life!"

Oh, and Honey, the laundry needs folding.

Remember, how you vowed to always do the laundry?

Looking For Direction

My husband and I are struggling to find direction.

I don't mean direction like agreeing on common values for our family, how we raise our kids, or where we will retire.

No, this struggle is far more immediate and somehow more challenging than that.

When I say we're struggling to find direction, I mean just that, or rather, find directions.

I know I'm only about a year into this marriage thing, so maybe you, Dear Reader, can help me here.

Is it just how the male and female brains are wired differently that we cannot agree on how to read directions?

How to get from here to there?

This should seem so easy in this new wonderful age of GPS. You simply plug where you want to go into your phone, it does that spinny thing where it figures out where you are, and Presto! You have directions!

Oh, were it only that simple.

This is exactly the point where the divide happens.

A philosophical difference greater than any religious conflict.

My husband's brain needs to look at a map. I need to look at written words.

"The directions say, 'Turn right at the next signal,'" I tell my husband as I navigate from the front passenger seat.

"Are you looking at the map?" he wants to know.

"No, I clicked on the icon that spells the direction out in words," I say.

"You have to look at the map," he insists, as if the typed directions will lead us only to Timbuktu.

"What do you care if I look at the map or the words?" I wonder. I don't get a sense of direction from a map. For him, words might as well be written in Portuguese.

"It has to be a map," he insists. "You need to follow the blue dot."

Ah, the dreaded Blue Dot, that flashing orb of misguided evil that promises it knows exactly where you are standing on the globe. Only it doesn't always get it right.

We're just back from a Thanksgiving trip where we cashed in a bunch of frequent flyer miles and took our teenaged girls to Paris and London. We relied on my husband, his smart phone and the dastardly Blue Dot to get us from place to place.

"It says it's only a 10-minute walk from the Eiffel Tower to Notre Dame," he promised. "C'mon let's walk and follow the Blue Dot."

I can't tell you how many alleged 10-minute walks turned into 45-minute marathons, all because the Blue Dot was off by more than just a few blocks. I honestly thought we were going to have a second French Revolution on the streets of Paris as our kids protested another Blue Dot adventure gone wrong.

"I can turn on my phone and ask for written directions," I offered.

That went over as well as a fallen chocolate soufflé. It's the oddest thing. My otherwise loving and reasonable husband would move the moon and stars for me, but asking him to give into written directions? I might as well have, well, asked a live human being for directions!

Somewhere out there, I'm sure there has to be a compromise, a way we can incorporate both maps and words. If you know where that is, maybe you can tell us how to get there, you know, send directions?

It is the issue that almost upended my marriage before it began.

I can picture you, Dear Reader, nodding your head in understanding. "Yes, it's tough to agree on religion, money, politics, how to raise our kids."

Actually, for two people raised in very different backgrounds, my husband and I are remarkably compatible when it comes to traversing those potential mine fields.

Our issue was, and can still be quite a tale.

Make that a tail.

And fur.

Bottom line, we don't share common values on animals.

My husband didn't grow up with pets, has no interest in animals, does not get the attraction.

Me? I'm that crazy animal wacko who was well on her way to becoming the eccentric cat lady down the street. Let me add, I was quite content with the idea of that.

He sees shedding, mess, and fleas.

I see unconditional love.

How did this happen? I've shared in this column how meticulous I was about making lists of the qualities I was looking for in a man.

I do remember the day we were introduced by mutual friends. This new person said something about not renting a house because "dogs had been living there."

"Oh, well, not my guy," I thought to myself.

When he asked me out for coffee a few weeks later, I made sure to out myself. "I have a dog, a 3-legged cat and just last week adopted four chickens," I shared.

He didn't run for the hills, so I figured his aversion to animals wasn't that strong. That he liked me for who I was.

That was a mistake.

After a couple years of dating and moving closer and closer to marriage, I could tell he was getting cold paws, er, feet.

"I just can't imagine living in a house with animals," he blurted during one emotional conversation. "I thought you had animals only as placeholders until you met, well, humans."

I hear my fellow animal lovers laughing and shaking their heads.

Not wanting to give up on each other, stubborn like two dogs on a bone, we headed to pre-marital counseling where we came to some agreements. We will always at least have one dog, probably no more cats, as my husband does have a mild allergy.

My big give was no more animals in our bedroom. My dog, Darla, now sleeps in our daughter's room. Almost everyone is thrilled with this arrangement, including our daughter who feels secure having a nice-sized protective dog sleeping by the side of her bed. Even Darla is happy, looking so proud at bedtime, prancing in our daughter's room like she's one of the big girls. She has a purpose.

Then there is me, who misses the sound of a dog snoring and licking her chops in her sleep, as she dreams of dancing cheeseburgers. Sounds that are as soothing to me as ocean waves crashing on a beach.

The sounds that give me joy these days? Eavesdropping on my husband. A year into our marriage, he's taken to having conversations with the animals when he thinks I'm not listening. "D-Dog, you love Daddy more than Mommy, right?" "Good Morning, Cat, you look happy today," are among the words I never thought he'd say.

Then there was the day a few weeks ago, when a couple of my chickens had died. Not knowing how to grieve a chicken, my wonderful husband blurted out, "Honey, you need to go restock."

Nothing says, "I love you," to an animal lover like, "Time to go get more chickens."

As I drove out to the country to pick out the new chicks I couldn't help but smile.

"I get to be the crazy animal lady AND have the husband and kid?" I thought.

Dreams really do come true.

When Marriage Means Learning To Love The Ugly

I did something this week I swore I would never do, managing to break not one, but two vows in the process.

And it's all part of the journey I share with you on a regular basis—what many of you have figured out before me—compromises you make as a wife and mother.

For this broken vow story, you and I must go back to my own childhood.

With four Jewish grandparents of varying degrees of observancy, we three Kagan children were raised what I would call, "mildly Jewish."

Sure, there were candles lit and gifts given on Hanukkah, and my parents saw nothing wrong with our sitting on Santa's lap or awaking on Christmas morning to find a stash of gifts.

The line of "it's not religious, if we decide it's not religious," stopped abruptly at what we kids thought was missing from the corner of our living room—a Christmas tree!

"If your grandfather walked in this house and saw a Christmas tree," our mother warned, "he would drop dead on the spot."

Nothing like effective parenting of raising your kids with a healthy dose of Jewish guilt. Not wanting Papa Harry to drop dead on the spot, we'd let the tree begging go until the next year.

Fast forward to my junior year of high school, when our beloved Papa Harry, did, indeed pass away. Come the next holiday season, we were sure we had the winning Christmas tree argument. "You can't say Papa Harry would drop dead," we pointed out so sensitively, "Because he did that last May."

"If your grandfather knew there was a Christmas tree in this house," Mom quickly replied, "he would roll over in his grave."

And so, the Christmas tree conversation appeared to be tabled for all time.

Until it wasn't.

Because once I became an adult, I could make my own choices. Rarely finding a holiday that I didn't love, I chose to embrace all the bright, shiny pieces of Christmas.

And so yes, I started putting up a tree. Sometimes small–ornaments hung from a palm tree in my small apartment when I was a newbie TV news reporter in Santa Barbara.

Sometimes over the top big, borrowing my friend Betsy's Ford F-150 pickup truck to get it home from the lot.

And so, I will never forget the early days of dating the man who is now my husband, walking into his home, that first Christmas, and seeing a "tree" that almost defies description.

He lost me at artificial.

"What about the wonderful smell from a fresh tree?" I asked.

"What about all the messy needles and the fire hazard?" he countered.

His tree wasn't just artificial. It glowed neon branches in colors I didn't even know existed, bursting out from fake snow encrusted plastic branches.

In a word, his tree was ugly.

"Never in my house," I vowed that first Christmas. "Should we marry, we will always have a fresh tree!"

And so here we are, married, living together. Busy lives, so much travel, multiple jobs, children, animals.

The thought of hauling off to the fresh tree lot is simply overwhelming.

"The messy needles," I caught myself complaining to no one but me. "The expense," added to the thought, "Y'know, there's that perfectly good tree down in the basement."

"How about this weekend you haul up your fake tree from the basement?" I asked my husband sweetly early this week.

He looked at me like aliens had invaded my brain.

"I thought you always wanted fresh?" he asked.

"Y'know, the expense, the mess. Besides, no one else in the world has your tree. Truly must be one of a kind."

Between you and me, I can't imagine they ever sold more than one of these things.

So, in one hauling of a tree, I've managed to offend my late grandfather and break a vow to my long-single self.

Talk about overachieving.

Once it was up, I did indeed see the ugly fake neon colors. There might be even more than last year. I think they spend 11-months of the year in the basement spontaneously reproducing.

The thing is, I now also see a one-stop shop. Plug it in you're done. And I see a symbol of how my husband did the best he could as a longtime single dad to the wonderful girl I'm now lucky enough to call my daughter.

That to me, makes the world's ugliest tree a thing of true holiday beauty.

Please tell me you've made similar holiday compromises?

See, I need something to tell my daughter.

"I thought you promised we'd have a fresh tree," she pointed out as she about passed out seeing the glowing plastic up in the corner of the living room.

"Uh, you're right, I did," I admitted. "Next year. I promise."

Lost Camera Captures The Hardest Part About Marriage

The answer is Buenos Aires, Argentina.

The question was, "Where will I spend the holidays?"

Faithful readers of this column know that up until the few days before Christmas I had no idea where that would be. In my last column, I shared how my new husband is an avid collector of frequent flyer miles and how using them often means spinning the wheel at the last second to see what's available.

He came up with South America. Even more than that, he pulled a last-second belated honeymoon out of a hat.

We danced tango at midnight, albeit quite clumsily. ("Dancing With the Stars" will not be calling anytime soon.)

We took an Argentine cooking class.

We floated away an afternoon on a boat on the Tigre Delta.

We had a ton of laughs as we took in the sights and sounds of Buenos Aires.

My husband took care of everything. Booking every tour, making every reservation, mapping out the entire last minute trip. For this lifetime single gal--I"ve gotten myself from Africa to Kuwait and back--it's was a new, fun, welcome experience to be taken care of.

Pretty much, my only job was to take the pictures. Which I did with great joy. That is, until the second to last night of the trip. That's when I let down my guard and left my beloved Nikon D100 SLR camera in the back of an Argentine taxi.

Chalk it up to the late hour, being tired. Whatever. No two ways about it. I blew it.

"I think I lost the camera," I said, feeling like I had the Rock of Gibraltar sinking in my stomach.

"It's gone?" my husband asked.

I explained how I hadn't seen it since we got in the taxi the night before. And it was nowhere to be found in any of my bags or around our hotel room.

That's how I get to the part of marriage I never anticipated and find a really don't like.

There's someone there to witness your mistakes.

It's like when you trip and fall in public. You might have smashed your nose or broken your wrist, but you know the first thing you do is look around to see if anyone just saw you make a fool of yourself.

I'm finding marriage is kind of like that. I certainly wasn't perfect when I was single. Messed up plenty of times. But then, it was just me to see it, to clean up the mess, to deal with the consequences.

Now there is someone to bear witness. Not jut someone, but my most important someone.

His reaction to this disturbing news was action, helping me search every corner of the room, checking in with front desk who looked at us like dumb Americans knowing that camera would never be seen again.

And with that, he let it go.

"Well, it's just stuff," he said.

"Just stuff?" I asked amazed. "But all of our pictures? The new zoom lens you just gave me? I had one job on this trip and I blew it."

He took my hand and said, "We're healthy. Our kids our healthy. The rest? It's just stuff."

That's how I ended up crying as we walked down the streets of Buenos Aires the last day of our trip.

Tears of embarrassment for blowing it; sad tears for losing one of the few material things I really care about; and tears of amazement of how I would get to bring home the best souvenir of all---a man who truly gets what's important.

Bad Pie

It would've been so easy to blame all this on my mother-in-law.

It was, after all, her chocolate pie recipe that reduced me to tears this week.

Like so many of my ill-fated ideas, this one started with what I thought were inspired, good intentions.

The challenge was our neighborhood's upcoming block party. Our house was to be the dessert stop. It was the first time our block has done this, and okay, I organized it and volunteered our house to be one of the stops. So, let's just get the blame out of the way.

No one to blame but myself.

For the party.

For the idea.

For the pressure of yes, trying to impress the neighbors.

"She writes, she runs a household, she organizes parties, and boy, can she bake!" I imagined them saying.

The question was, "What to bake?" It needed to be good. And if it were to please my own family, it needed to be chocolate.

"Chocolate. Chocolate. Chocolate?" I wracked by brain when it came to me.

My mother-in-law's chocolate pie.

This is no ordinary chocolate pie.

From the day I met my husband and daughter they have waxed poetic about "Gommie's Chocolate Pie." How it's the chocolatiest, best ever pie ever.

With only a year of marriage under my belt, dare I ask for the recipe?

"I have a big ask," I said as I phoned small town Texas.

"Yes?" My mother-in-law replied.

"Would you be willing to share your chocolate pie recipe?"

The chuckle in her voice told me she was thrilled I wasn't calling with bad news and being the generous soul that she is, that she would love to share. And so, she started firing off the list of ingredients and instructions. "And this part is so easy," she instructed. "You make the filling in microwave. You don't even bother with getting a pot dirty."

"Perfect!" I said thanking her profusely. Easy and no mess. Exactly what I was looking for.

Until, I started.

The chocolate filling should've thickened after a few minutes in the microwave..

It did not.

The less it thickened, the more I zapped.

The more I zapped, the less it thickened.

I launched into battle with this chocolate goo.

Until I gave up and poured what was left of this reduced lump of gummy brown glue into the pie shell.

It filled up about a third of the crust.

"This is terrible!" my family exclaimed. "What are these lumps?"

I think I made my husband homesick for his Mommy.

As my family laughed away at my chocolate disaster, I excused myself and went upstairs and cried.

Not so much because of the pie. More because I'd been found out.

Have you ever had a dream come true, only to know deep down you probably don't deserve it?

My new family now knew the truth about me. All because of this chocolate pie.

See, even though I now make dinner every night, my dirty little secret is I don't know how to cook.

Well, for most of my life I didn't know. It was so bad, my immediate family only let me do dishes on Thanksgiving.

About five years ago, I started with small training wheel kind of steps, like trying recipes for one in a crock pot. By time I met my future husband three years ago, I could pass as someone who could kind of cook.

But this disaster of a chocolate pie brought it all back. Like the fat person who lost 400 pounds, looks in the mirror and still sees fat.

Maybe this is the real me. Someone who can't make a simple chocolate pie. Maybe I'm meant to be a lonely single girl after all.

Yes, from here, this all might sound dramatic. You, however, didn't see the pile of chocolate goo.

I wiped my tears and called my mother-in-law to say, "Thanks," and assure her that she remains Queen of the Chocolate Pie.

"Maybe some time when you visit I can stand beside you and watch how you do it?" I suggested.

"I'd love that," she said. Told you she's generous.

As for dessert, I went to the supermarket, bought a cake from their bakery, ice cream, and fixin's for sundaes.

Store bought? Turns out the neighbors were so impressed that I made things so simple.

I Got In Bed With A Stranger Last Night

There was a stranger in my bed last night.

Goodness, what would my husband say?

Thing is, this man looked an awful lot like the guy I married a couple of years ago.

Except for one thing.

This man was wearing-

Was wearing—

Reading glasses.

I can barely get out the words.

Judge? Me?

No way. I've been wearing those suckers for a few years now.

My husband?

He's fought it.

Maybe it's pride.

Maybe the fact he's four years younger, didn't want to admit he was going, you know, *there*.

He fought by it pulling over a candle to read the menu in a dimly lit restaurant.

By occasionally, asking to borrow my reading glasses for some tedious task.

Apparently, the day came this week where he could fight no more.

Of course, being my husband, he found a way to order online for very little money and earn a zillion airline miles.

He can see fine print and we'll no doubt be flying off somewhere.

It's helped him accept this new development.

Sadly, you get what you pay for in terms of style.

These glasses are huge and, what's the word?

That's right—ugly.

They look like he borrowed them from Mike Brady on one of the later episodes of "The Brady Bunch."

So much for Husband who swore he would do without.

"You sure are wearing those new glasses a lot," I commented to the stranger in my bed. "I thought you didn't need them?"

"Father Time is undefeated," he said accepting his visual fate.

And there you have it.

Why this moment that I had thought would be so satisfying, that sense of "Welcome to the Club," is instead a tiny bit unsettling.

It's the first time I've seen my husband age.

It's like when you haven't seen a parent for a few months and notice their step or thoughts are a touch slower.

It's like seeing all those old people on Facebook who look like the parents of the kids we grew up with, only to realize, "Holy Moly! Those aren't the parents, those ARE the people we grew up with!"

Which leads me back to the stranger in my bed.

He was my husband with a sprinkling of Father Time.

The discovery of this slightly older man all makes this marriage thing all the more profound.

There's this reminder in this other person. We are going to age. Shoot, we are aging. Thing is, we're doing together.

It's pretty bittersweet.

Maybe you see it in your spouse, Dear Reader.

In your kid, who suddenly looks older in a photograph.

At your high school reunion.

Father Time, indeed, is not denied.

Our loved ones are our reminders and our comfort.

As for the whole, "It's so sexy to find a stranger in my bed!" idea, picture the Mike Brady glasses and you'll have the answer to that question.

My only hope—Husband doesn't realize these baby strength glasses will only serve him a short while.

Thank goodness for Father Time. Stronger lenses and hipper frames just might be around the corner.

The Key To Finding Lost Keys

"We have a crisis going on here."

Those are not exactly the words you want to hear from your daughter when you're calling home from the other side of the country.

"I've only been gone a few hours. What could possibly have gone wrong?" I asked with a jillion scenarios racing through my mind.

"Daddy can't find his keys," my daughter explained.

"Oh," was all I could say, at first simultaneously giving thanks that that was all it was, and an "Uh oh," realizing this was going to get ugly before it got better.

And so begins this tale of an upside down obstacle, Dear Reader, that I bet you can relate to—

What do you do when you've lost that item you absolutely must have?

For my husband it was his car keys.

"No big deal," I think I might've heard you smirking, except that we are talking the added stress of the missing wife, (that would be me at a speaking gig on the other side of the country) and the dreaded Small Window.

Trying-To-Show-He-Can-Do-It-All Husband had only minutes after picking our daughter up from school. He needed to walk the dog, throw dinner together, and was getting ready to go to his baseball game.

Yes, baseball game. As in yes, he plays baseball. Not softball. Baseball. As in yes, he's too old to be putting his body through that, as in—that's a whole other column.

"I've looked in the car, on the street, on our bed, in the laundry—"

"He's digging in our neighbor's trash," my daughter chimed in.

"I cleaned out the freezer," he added.

"The freezer? You thought you left your keys in the freezer?" I asked, in my not so helpful voice. "And?"

"Not there," Husband grumbled.

"Bummer," said me, the useless long distance wife. "But, hey, thanks for getting that freezer cleaned out. It's been on my 'To Do' list for months."

There I was, going all gratitudey on him. My friend, Lisa, likes to say that in a crisis we all revert to type.

I went spiritual.

"You need to turn it over to Saint Anthony," I instructed from Los Angeles. "He's the saint of lost items."

"We're not Catholic," my dubious husband countered.

"You want to split hairs or find your keys?"

"Well, I did say, 'Kallan, Kallan, Kallan,'" he said, invoking my younger sister's name.

"She's our Parking Fairy, not The Lost Key Saint," I explained.

It does happen to be true that saying my sister's name three times will always produce the best spot in any crowded parking lot, but again—that's a different story. Try it for yourself. For the record, she's useless when it comes to finding lost keys.

With the clock ticking, the pressure mounting, and the big game looming, my husband went full-on conspiracy theory.

"I think the mailman stole them or I left them in the front door and someone came up and grabbed them," he opined.

I know our daughter was rolling her eyes at that one as much as I was. Her corner when things go bad–declare her parents are nuts. "Robbing mailman, praying to saints, you people are crazy."

I can't say she was wrong about that.

Turns out Husband never did make it his baseball game that night, which might not be such a bad thing.

And I never did hear how he was planning on getting to work the next day.

In the end, the key to the keys, the savior, the answer turned out to be simple, total exhaustion.

With not a single drop of energy left, Husband crawled into bed where, you guessed it-his leg kicked a lump of a metal object.

There were his keys.

"I swear I checked the bed 10 times!" he declared when recounting the happy moment.

Doesn't it always work that way? Be it lost keys or love or the meaning of life, you don't find the thing you're looking for so desperately until you totally give up.

How does it work for you, Dear Reader? How do you find lost items you must have?

My husband would love to chime in, but he's busy—writing a letter of apology. Needs to say he's sorry for slandering our perfectly nice mailman.

"Taking off for Hong Kong in Singapore Airlines First Class Cabin.
Tickets would've cost $27,000. Husband paid $20 a piece."

As husband problems go, this is not one likely elicit much sympathy.

I get that.

So, you know the kind of man who loves to travel, see the world, whisk his wife away on romantic adventures across the globe?

Yeah, I got one of those.

"And the problem is——?" you ask.

The problem is, as long as you asked, I like to stay home.

Home, as in with my kids, my pets, my crazy neighbors, fuzzy socks, my routine.

I spent much of a 20-years-plus news career with a packed suitcase ready to fly out the door.

Which was great.

These days, I rarely get a traveling itch thinking, "Gee, wish I was there instead of here."

Meanwhile, together, Husband and I have been to South America, Asia, Europe, and Dominican Republic together, just to name a few hot spots.

Nothing makes his heart go aflutter more than taking off for a foreign land.

See, Husband has this rather nerdy hobby of collecting frequent flyer miles by the way we spend our money. Your eyes would cross to see his formula of credit cards, online shopping portals, and following other crazies who write blogs and Twitter feeds about such topics.

"Got us two first-class tickets to Italy," he announced recently as pleased with himself as he had slain a dragon.

"How much did you pay?" I asked knowing this is his favorite question.

"Well, they should've cost about $20,000," he started off.

"And?"

"And I paid $140 for both!" he exclaimed. Make sure you insert, "Giggling like a schoolgirl," when you try to imagine him saying this.

And so, off we went to the land of romance, pasta, and fresh tomatoes.

"How are you doing?" my sister texted me as Husband and I changed planes.

"I think, I'm turning into more of a homebody as I get older," I confessed.

"Please," she corrected. "You were a homebody when you were eight."

Ah, yes the vivid memory of Montecito Sequoia Girls Camp.

So homesick I could barely breathe.

True story—I wrote a letter home to my parents using felt tip ink and held the paper under my chin so that my tears could splash the page and make the ink run.

You laugh, but hey, it worked. My parents came and got me. To this day, they're convinced that something awful must have happened at that camp.

Nothing bad ever happened.

Except, I wanted to come home.

Flash forward all these decades later. There was no calling my Mommy as I flew over the Atlantic with the man I love.

Enjoying Rome and the Amalfi Coast was pretty darn easy.

Once my husband gets me out there, he and I are well-matched travel companions in what we want to do, see, eat and spend.

Husband, sensing my delight with the trip, thinking just maybe he had converted me from "stayer" to "goer," took my hand, smiled and asked, "So where do you want to go next?"

I could see he was hoping for "Ireland! Morocco! Capetown!"

It broke my heart to have to break his.

"Home," I confessed. "I want to go home."

The day after our return Husband says, "Y'know, I'm happy to be home, too."

A small white lie on his part?

Perhaps.

But a man who loves to see me happy? That's someone I'll follow to the ends of the Earth.

Is Husband's Surprise A Good Thing?

To be surprised? Or not surprised?

That is the marital question I need your help with this week, Dear Reader. I've shared in previous columns my husband's rather quirky, geeky hobby. Crazy, mad genius obsession, might be a better description.

Husband collects frequent flyer miles without flying.

Millions of them.

It's all the way we spend our money: mortgage, power bill, grocery store, clothes.

No dollar goes out the door without generating miles. Make that multiples of miles.

We live by spread sheets, blogs, Twitter feeds, all tipping him off to the latest deal to multiply the miles.

Before you ask for more details, let me say, our home is "Crazyland."

"Never heard back from your friend, Judy," Husband mentioned after he sent her his introductory single-spaced mad-scientist miles explainer.

"Remember the movie, 'Jerry Maguire,'" I told him. "You had me at 'Hello?'"

"Sure."

"You lost her at 'expect to spend 8-10 hours a week pursing this hobby.'"

He still doesn't get how funny that line is to normal folks.

His craziness does mean we usually take at least two big trips a year.

For this year's Grown Ups only trip, Husband is whisking me off to the Maldives.

Yeah, I had to look it up on a map, too.

Basically, it's one of those magical huts over clear blue water kind of places on the other side of the world. We're flying some super luxurious airline over there. I think we get our room or something crazy like that.

The tickets just to get there would coast $45,000.

I kid you not.

Husband paid $7 a piece.

Again.

Not kidding.

Seven bucks.

Yep, life with Crazy Husband has its perks.

The challenge is the way back.

We are stopping somewhere on the way home.

Allegedly as fantastic as the Maldives.

Husband doesn't want to tell me where.

"This will be so romantic," he insists. "A surprise."

He laughs when he says this because he also knows it tests my desire, to well, control things.

Gasp!

Husband being great husband doesn't want to be too tortuous, so this week he made an offer.

"I'll tell you where we're going," he said. "if it will help you relax and have a better time."

So there it is—offer on the table.

My question to you, Dear Reader, should I find out now? Blow the surprise, but ease my international travel butterflies?

Or do I go with the flow and pretend this is, what's the word he used, oh that's right. "Fun."

Our girls will be with my sister and her wife. They will be so well taken care of and spoiled at "Aunt Camp" that their only worry will be that our trip doesn't last longer. And all the aunts, adults outside of me will have an exact itinerary of where we are headed.

To know or not to know?

That is my challenge and question to you this week.

You Could Call This The Worst Anniversary Dinner Ever

You could've called it the worst anniversary dinner ever.

This week, Husband and I were excited to celebrate our third wedding anniversary.

Yes, can you believe it?

It's already been three years since this forever-single lady found a perfectly imperfect man who wanted to spend his life with me.

We had reservations at a fancy, new restaurant in town. And sure, we could've gone there had drinks and the latest "farm-to-table" dishes.

At the last minute, we looked at each other with a shared streak of rebellion. "Let's ditch this predictable Popsicle stand and head for an adventure."

We pulled up an article featuring a list of authentic, ethnic restaurants we've been wanting to try.

That's how we ended up at a little hole-in-the-wall Mom n'Pop Korean restaurant about a half-hour away.

Things went goofy from the start.

As soon as we were seated, the server ran up to our table. "You should try the seafood pancake!" she insisted, pointing to the item on the menu written mainly in Korean. "A man ordered the wrong pancake. Doesn't want it. You eat it."

Before we knew what was happening, the steaming, previously untouched, unwanted pancake was sitting in front of us with side dishes known as "banchan."

It was delicious.

Meanwhile, we ordered the special chicken dish mentioned in article that alerted us to this restaurant.

We waited.

And waited.

And waited.

"So sorry," the server apologized when she came back a half hour later. "Chef cooked your food. I give it to someone else. I'll make you another one!"

And with that, she was off giving us no chance to protest.

So we waited again.

While we were waiting, I took the chance to ask Husband, "So how has the first three years of marriage gone for you?"

I asked knowing he could call this the marriage from hell.

There's my old stinky dog, raising teenagers, my obsession with finishing my first novel, my ailing elderly mother on the other side of the country. All things that often get my attention ahead of him.

"This marriage has far exceeded my wildest expectations," he smiled, taking my hand.

Does he not see all my flaws and our challenges?

Because let me assure you, they are on full display every day.

He says he sees a wife who doesn't nag, who is a great mom, who travels the world with him, and laughs at about a third of his really bad puns.

I see a man who is incredibly generous with what he chooses to see.

Which brings me back to that darn chicken.

It finally came.

A huge mound of steaming chicken, rice noodles, chiles and spices.

I have to say it far exceeded our wildest expectations.

So yes, you could call it the worst anniversary dinner ever.

I'd call it perfect.

A reminder and celebration of life.

So often you can't control what you get served up or when it arrives.

And a crazy chicken dish, like the right wonderfully imperfect man sure is worth waiting for.

The Only Wedding Present We Wanted

The box awaits.

It's not fancy by any means.

A cardboard box from a craft store that my friend's 10-year-old daughter decorated with decals and quotes about love.

It is simply the best wedding gift my husband and I received.

It's pretty much the only wedding gift my husband and received.

There's that.

It's how we wanted it.

We got married in our late 40's, already had two households of stuff. Asking our friends for more stuff just seemed silly.

To us, anyway.

So we asked our friends and family for this.

The treasures inside the box.

Dear Reader, you might remember that Husband and I got married twice.

The first, was our quickie, legal wedding. We didn't want to just live together. So, we grabbed our girls, hired an officiant and headed to a waterfall two hours away.

It was perfect.

And, I still wanted "the wedding."

So two months later, we gathered with friends and family in the backyard of a friend who had a gorgeous home.

It was a "no presents" affair.

I mean really.

Except for one thing.

That box.

As guests walked into the festivities, they found a table with different colored cards and envelopes numbered 1-10.

"Please write us a note, a greeting, some advice," we asked. "Put your note in an envelope and we will open it on the anniversary of corresponding number."

Talk about the gift that keeps on giving.

Each year on September 15th, we take the box down from a shelf in our den and open the envelopes with the number matching that anniversary.

I think it's even better than looking at photos or videos.

It's like having that special person with you in the den.

Year One included a note from the parents of my husband's late first wife.

"We believe you'll have many happy memories from this first year. Thank you for including us in your family," they wrote. Talk about a reminder of the fabric of our family.

A Year Two envelope revealed a note from a dear college friend who is now a minister.

"May laughter dance in your presence

May strength be in your ties

May the Lord hold you tightly

May each day hold surprise."

Year Two also had this gem from my friend and pet sitter, Heidi, "I hope your pack has grown by leaps and bounds!"

Nice thought, but the fact that it hasn't, that we are capped off with one dog, one 3-legged cat and six chickens in the backyard, is why we have made it to anniversary #3.

Whose notes await us?

Only the box knows.

We'll find out each year on September 15th.

And if we're blessed enough to make it to Year 11, we'll start over with the envelopes marked for Year One.

We're not special.

I suspect you might be over "stuff," as well.

For about $20, this kind of treasure can be yours, too.

A box, some inexpensive stationary, and some pens for your guests.

That's all it takes for a surprise box of memories to await on your shelf.

My Happy Marriage That Surely Will Not Last

Of all the punch lines I never planned on, this must surely be it.

Somehow, I, out of all people, wake up today on the third anniversary of being married to a perfectly imperfect man.

A man with more quirks than a roomful of brilliant physicists.

After all, what could be quirkier than a man who loves me and treats me with such kindness and respect?

Yeah, me.

The forever-single gal who must've dated every non-commital man in America.

Yeah, me, who was a bridesmaid so many times I finally had to retire.

That fifth peach-colored dress did me in.

Yeah, me, who has been a third wheel so many times I could open my own tire store.

Yeah, me, who looks around and sees so many of my long-married friends going through divorces or seemingly stuck in unhappy marriages and relationships.

I'm the one with the great guy?

As I cue the laugh track, I'm in no way being cocky, just clear.

I now know that all those break-ups, heartaches, lonely times were not my ending.

Just like I know my marriage to my wonderfully imperfect man is not my happy ending.

It is simply my right now.

Now is pretty great.

Gotta say.

And,

Now can end at any moment.

I know my happy marriage surely will not last.

It will end, just as everything ends, as in the natural order of things.

Gotta always remember that.

We are not a perfect couple.

There's that.

We can stumble, as others have.

One of us can get sick.

One will most probably die before the other.

Skip the stupid "Life, spouse, kid, job is perfect" posts on social media.

Instead, read the folks keeping it real.

You'll see that stuff happens.

I share today, on our third wedding anniversary, to say to my perfectly imperfect husband, "Thank you for our now. You sure took a long time to get here. And boy, were you worth waiting for."

And, to you.

You, who is reading this waiting for your better now.

Good gosh, it can happen.

If it can happen to me, it can happen to anyone.

If I had the magic formula how, I'd be sharing that, making a billion bucks.

What I can tell you, what I promise, as you wait, this is not the end of your story.

It's simply your now.

And when that better one arrives, you better cherish it, appreciate it, and love it for the better now it surely will be, for however long it lasts.

Happy Third Anniversary, Husband. Looking forward to every single day we are lucky enough to have now.

Parenting

Thinking of Someone Special On My First Mother's Day

I think about her every day.

We are forever linked through one of the greatest joys of my life.

And I'll never be able to tell her.

That's what I find myself thinking about this, my first Mother's Day as a mother.

I'll never be able to say, "Thank you" to the woman who started the job I'm blessed to continue.

She is my daughter's other mother.

I've shared here in this column how I've recently come to motherhood in a rather unconventional way.

A few years ago I started dating a single dad who was raising his daughter alone. She was 8-years-old when her mom died. 11-years-old when we met.

Last summer, her dad and I got married and this spring we completed our adoption.

There are no "step, half, kinda" or any other qualifiers in our home. I am a full-fledged, lunch-making, laundry-folding, carpool driving, full-time mother. Though, I like to joke about the drudgery, the truth is, being a mom is a lifetime wish I had long ago let go of coming true.

And yet, I never forget the bittersweet twist, for my daughter's first mother. Her loss, the loss of her young life, ends up being my gain.

I'm clear that I'm not here to replace her. Rather, this motherhood journey is one we will forever share.

I watch old family videos and see my daughter learning to walk, lunging into her mother's arms. I hear them giggling when she says calls dinner "chicken stoob" instead of chicken stew. When she pats her mother's throbbing head saying, "Mommy has a hairache."

If I could meet my daughter's other mother, I would share that when my husband tells our girl she has a trait "you get that from Mommy," or "That's just like your Mom," she lights up with pride. We all know who he's talking about.

And it's not me.

I'm fine with this. My motherhood bucket already overflows with so much more than I ever thought I'd get to experience.

I'm now the one to tuck her in at night, to talk about boys, to shop for her dress for the upcoming end of year school dance. That's she and I cuddling on the couch as we watch American Idol. That was my lap she was sitting on a few weeks ago when I let her steer the car down our quiet street. "You're definitely going to be the one to teach me to drive," she announced assessing who will be calmer, me or her father.

Those are the joys I get to have instead of her mom who left too soon.

"My school bus driver thinks I look more like you than Daddy," she shared one day recently, seeming to relish the connection between us.

We got a big giggle out of that one, especially since we truly look nothing alike. I'm tall and have a dark complexion. She's short and has skin as light and pure as a porcelain doll with blue eyes that someone recently told her look like two deep swimming pools.

The truth is, the one she looks like the most right now is her grandfather, her Pops, her other mother's father. As she grows she's looking more and more like the beautiful young woman I see in the photo that hangs in her bedroom.

It was the first photo I hung when we all moved in together last summer. "I like to have pictures of people I love hanging in my home," I explained to my new daughter. "And even though I never got to meet your mom, she's one of my best friends simply because she made you."

I'm thinking about the seven Mothers Days my daughter's first mother was able to have, realizing on this, my first, none is promised to us.

Were I able to send her a card, I would write, "Thank you, for sharing this incredible journey with me. Together, we are raising one awesome girl."

Why Didn't Someone Warn Me Before I Adopted My Daughter?

If I'd only known.

Somehow, I thought by adopting a full-sized kid I would avoid biological changes to my body.

Silly me.

I met my daughter when she was 11. We finalized the adoption earlier this year.

No, there were no post-pregnancy pounds to lose, as I had my figure back within minutes of signing those papers.

I can't blame any stretch marks on my body on pregnancy. Those were of my own making.

But there is one key biological change I never expected that has taken over my body, mind, and soul.

Since becoming a mother, I have become a crier.

Yes, crier.

Just ask my daughter. Making me tear up and cry is as easy as flipping on the kitchen sink.

Watching my daughter get on the school bus and drive away on the first day of school—you'd thought I was watching the sappiest TV movie of the week the way the tears poured down my cheeks.

Seeing her gather nice girlfriends for a simple birthday party. Let's just say it's a good thing I wasn't near the candles on the cake. My tears would've put out the flames and made for a soggy mess.

Going to her first school football game with my husband and her, just like my dad used to take me and my siblings—oh boy. Tried to hold on until a big play so I could nonchalantly wipe away tears while standing up to cheer the team.

"Why do you always have to cry?" my daughter wants to know, which is usually followed by "You're so weird."

I get her not getting it. I certainly didn't get it when I was her age. Shoot, I didn't get it well into my 40's before I got her. I, too, used to look at my friends who are moms and criers and silently think to myself, "You're so weird."

But now I know to be a mom, or maybe simply a parent, no matter how or when you become one, is to love someone outside of yourself and to be so excited for all that is before them and all that is possible. That, is what I suspect triggers the tears. A trigger so strong it feels like it must be mommy biology at work.

There we were in the post office the other day–My daughter and I applying for her passport.

Uh oh. I could fill the tear tank filling up.

"You're going to cry? Here? Really?" My daughter was not pleased. "It's a form. A really bad picture of me. It's a post office!"

"That's what you see," I told her. "I see the years flying by. In about two minutes you'll be a college student with a knapsack over your shoulder backpacking across Europe, having the time of your life."

Yeah, so I almost lost it in the middle of the post office. I bit the inside of my cheek, focused on checking the boxes. I actually kind of held it together.

So, if you're thinking about adopting, I'm telling you what no one told me. The biological changes, the tears—they are a comin'.

If I'd only known.

The idea that I could love someone so much and get so much joy out of taking care of another person?

If I'd only known. Truth is, I probably would've cried.

The Pre-Cry

"Did you cry?"

There you have the number one thing my daughter wanted to know, as she quizzed me like I was a guilty suspect and she was a top detective on CSI.

Truth is, I can't really blame her.

As I've shared with you Dear Reader, since becoming a parent, I've become a crier.

If you ask my kids, they will tell you that I cry at the most ridiculous times.

I cried when one filled out form for a passport.

To think—the adventures the world will show her!

Cried when another jumped off the high dive for first time.

Oh, the courage!

The family stories go on and on.

There we were last weekend at Daughter's first ever cross country meet.

Daughter who, how shall we say this, is not the fastest cougar in the jungle.

Daughter who, how shall we say this, we weren't very confident she could finish the entire 3.1 mile race without stopping.

I could easily make the case there would be grounds for crying as I saw her---

Facing something daunting and scary, wearing her school colors for the first time, running cross country like I did when I was in high school.

I thought about my daughter's question.

And confessed.

"Well, I pre-cried," I said.

"You pre-cried?" she rolled her eyes in the horror of my never-ending mother weirdness.

Dear Reader, do your tears, too, have a clock of their own?

"As I walked and scouted the course before you ran, I had a moment," I explained to my daughter.

"A moment?"

"Well, a few moments, actually, where I pictured you putting one foot in front of the other, of pumping your arms, of not giving up, just like we talked about. And yeah, I got choked up thinking about it. I cried then."

"And during the actual race?"

"Honestly, I got so busy cheering you on, taking pictures, and running from one point to the next to see you as many times as possible that I think I forgot to cry during the actual race."

"So you pre-cried," my husband asked me later that day.

"You heard about that?"

"Oh, it's already part of family legend," he smiled. "The Pre-Cry."

In another life, i.e., when I was single, I suppose I would've been embarrassed.

But being married and a mom means no emotion is your own. It's all out there for the family to see, naked as a plucked turkey on Thanksgiving morning.

And now it is with you, Dear Reader.

You, who I bet understands the concept of a pre-cry, how the very thought of something emotional can turn on the water works before an actual event takes place.

And you, who I bet understands the post-cry, as well: Tears that come long after.

Long after saying goodbye to someone you love.

Long after making it through an obstacle you once couldn't see your way around.

Did I mention my daughter finished the race without stopping?

I'm afraid I have to wrap it up here.

I feel a post-cry coming on.

My parents' chiding still rings in my head.

"Daryn, you need to learn to share your favorite doll and toys with your little sister."

Ah, memories of being 8-years-old and still learning how to share.

From my "I'm all grown up now" vantage point, I have to say—this sharing thing is a ridiculous concept.

As if you're supposed to be happy about loaning out your most prized treasure. Try on the grown up version of that—How about your girlfriend saying, "I love your diamond engagement ring! Can I wear it for a week?" Or "I love your house! Can you move out and let me live there for a year?"

Y'know. You gotta share.

It strikes me with a twist of bittersweet irony, that a year into marriage, I find the treasure I'm now expected to share is, in fact, my younger sister.

What a busy 18 months it has been! My sister and I have both gotten married for the first time. We're living 1,000 miles apart, consumed with jobs and all that comes with new families.

"Do you realized we haven't seen each other in a year?" I asked her the other day, stating what would've been an inconceivable idea in the past. "How did that happen?"

I'm probably biased, but I think this is no ordinary sisters' relationship, as we've had more than our share of quality sister time. It's one of the underappreciated aspects of a very extended singlehood (fancy words for not getting married until I was 49.) For many years, my younger sister and I took trips together and celebrated holidays. We had countless hours to share, giggle and confess our darkest fears.

True quality sister time.

Oh, how I was looking forward to more of that as we began to plan her upcoming visit.

"I don't think it would be a good idea if you guys spend the *whole* day together when she comes to visit," my new daughter suggested the other day. "Because that would be like, her whole trip."

Instead she and our other child, my Little Sister in the Big Brother Big Sister program, have planned a weekend full of haunted house visits, manicures, and shopping.

"You can come, too," was my daughter's attempt at sharing. "But just know she's really coming to see us."

It sure does make my heart swell to see this relationship grow. I just haven't become a wife and mother. My sister has become an aunt.

"Best gift you ever gave me," she told me on my wedding day. "Growing our family."

She's not just an aunt. She's "Aunt Of The Century." She's hosted the girls at her cabin in The Catskills. There have been trips to amusement parks. And the simple gesture of staying connected with phone calls and texts.

To my girls, my sister has become, sigh, a treasure.

Our treasure.

And so we countdown to her upcoming visit when we will share.

My antidote for the small slice of my sister's time I will have that weekend? She and I have planned yet another weekend in November when we will fly to see our mother on her birthday.

"Why aren't we all going?" my daughter wanted to know.

Sorry, Kid. This one is my turn. Well, and my mom's. Won't she be so proud how well she taught me to share?

"On a Sisters' trip Annecy, France. Just to have a turn with my sissy by myself."

The New Neighbor Has My Daughter Packing Her Things

Leave it to my young, teenaged daughter to succinctly describe a scene from the sitcom that is sometimes my life.

"That awkward moment when you discover your gynecologist is moving in next door," she said as she slid down in horror in the front passenger seat of my car.

There is some teenager embellishment in that statement. My gynecologist of more than 15 years is not moving in next door.

It's more like three doors down.

I made this discovery as I was driving down the street the other day, kid in tow, and came upon two images I couldn't quite put together in my head. There was the house that has been for sale for the last four months and standing right in front, holding a tape measure, was indeed, my gyno.

"What are you doing here?" I asked as I rolled down my car window.

"We're buying this house!" he smiled with all the excitement of a new homeowner. "It's exactly what we've been looking for."

"Oh, wow, welcome," I said. "Don't know if you realize, but I live down the block. Oh, and that new patient I referred to your practice? She's two doors down."

"Great." He seemed unfazed. "Like a satellite office."

Out of the corner of my eye, I saw my daughter sliding down in her seat, trying to make herself invisible.

"Awkward!" she declared as we drove away. "We need to move!"

Of course, when you're 14, the very idea of the gynecologist is disgusting. Hey, the annual visit is hardly the highlight of the year for most of us big girls. Add to that, the idea that we will now have to pass his house in order to get to ours.

"He's seen you 'down there' everyday!" she groaned.

"Not every day, just once a year," I corrected, finding myself at one of those ongoing challenging moments we mothers of girls face.

Everything, it seems is a potential message about how we feel about our bodies. One misstep, the experts and blogs warn, and your kid is headed straight to an eating disorder.

"Don't talk about hating your body," they admonish. "Don't talk about being fat or anything else negative concerning her body."

Really? After she downs her third blueberry muffin and hasn't gotten up off the couch for any physical activity for weeks, I'm just supposed to smile at her like she's a perfect health angel?

Where's the line?

Healthy body image vs. realistic and important health choices?

Fortunately, in the case of the new neighbor, I had a good answer.

"Parts is parts," I said nonchalantly. "I don't have anything 'down there' he hasn't seen on thousands of women every single day for the last 30 years."

Don't give me too much credit. I'm not so progressive that I would *start* going to a gynecologist I knew first as a neighbor. But this particular doc is like gold. I've had his cell phone number for years. I can text him if I don't feel well on a weekend or to refill a prescription. You know how rare that is? Even more rare than a good neighbor, which I'm sure he's going to be. So feet in the stirrups once a year for the guy down the block it will be.

"Sure will make next month's Block Party all the more interesting," I joked to my daughter.

"You're really weird," she declared.

I smiled.

Your teen tells you "You're weird," you know you must be doing something right.

Do you think the new neighbors will notice?

Mommy Outfit of Shame

In case you were wondering—

The lady running around last weekend from one end of the metro area to the other in what can best be described as "Mom High Fashion of Shame?"

Yeah, that was me.

How shall I best describe my outfit?

T shirt that I had slept in, so big it would still be loose on King Kong. Sweats from 1984, or thereabouts with stains and holes to match. Plastic Croc sandals. Uncombed hair half up in a clip.

Teeth were brushed. Yay for me. Points for that.

Bra? Deodorant? I managed one. You can figure out which. Let's just say you wouldn't have wanted to come too close.

How did I manage to (as I hear my own mother's voice shrilling in my head,) ever let myself "go out of the house looking like that?!"

I can explain in one word:

Karma.

I'll admit it.

I was that long-time single gal who had "tsk tsk'ed" other women, mothers, leaving the house looking like a hot mess just to get their kids where they needed to go.

"I'll never do that, if I'm ever a mother," I said silently. Smugly.

Clearly, we make plans. The Fashion Gods laugh.

How did I step out in the Mommy Outfit of Shame?

Would you believe I thought I was leaving the house for a simple 5-minute drop-off at the school close to our house?

It's what I do every weekday—transition from sleep to taxi service by throwing something on the bottom of fancy (not) giant sleep shirt.

Would you believe that simple 5-minute drop off turned into a 5-hour comedy errors where, as they say in local news, "Something went terribly wrong?"

There I was Saturday morning. All I needed to do was get one of our kids to school so she could hop on a bus to her cross country meet.

When the bus wasn't there, we figured we'd missed it, so I decided to drive the kid to the actual meet, which happened to be more than an hour away.

Or so we thought.

It took two more stops to get to the actual correct location.

And so yes, that was me.

The awful looking bag lady frantically driving across the state and back looking for a meet, running into countless people I knew along the way.

The lesson in this?

Not being attached to how I look?

That the kid is more important?

That, dare I say this, my mother is right?

I really shouldn't leave the house looking like that even for five minutes.

I've learned a lot in the last few years jumping into this Mommy Land.

You've been kind, Dear Reader, to not let me know this badge was waiting for me.

Motherhood doesn't get more embarrassing than this?

Rather, better you don't tell me.

Let's keep it to sharing your horrifying Mommy Moment you thought would never come.

Or even, worse, how your mother was right.

The Way Thanksgiving Is Supposed To Taste

Here it comes.

The family strife.

The mess of our differences.

All found

At the bottom

Of a casserole dish.

I'm talking, Dear Reader, about

Thanksgiving

And

Sweet potatoes.

How do you love yours?

Are your sweet potatoes mashed?

In a pie?

Squished into a casserole dish?

Dare I even broach a topic more prickly than some which have divided nations?

I will only whisper the word--topping.

"To marshmallow or not to marshmallow? That is the question."

Because we share these things, you and I, I will tell I'm about to smash head onto one of the most disappointing things about my family.

For years, I dreamed of having my own family, making Thanksgiving Dinner. Of course, the centerpiece would the dish that I grew up looking forward to all year long.

My mother's sweet potato casserole.

Her sweet potatoes are a sugar shock hot mess of wonderfulness.

They start with giant cans of candied yams, smashed into submission with tons of brown sugar, butter, a little bit of orange rind to give it some zip and crushed pineapple to add to the texture and make it even sweeter.

All that gets baked in a giant casserole dish and the piece de resistance—topped with giant melted marshmallows.

To eat it is to love it and put on about 12 pounds per serving.

The first time I made it for my husband and kids was a life moment come true.

Only one problem.

They hated it.

Hated it!

It has become a family joke how much they hate my beloved dish.

"Who puts pineapple in sweet potatoes?" is the never-ending punch line.

Stop by our house around Easter, they'll still be laughing about my sweet potatoes from Thanksgiving.

It hurts, yet I know I'm not any better than they are.

None of us are.

Dear Reader, don't you have a certain way your holiday food is supposed to taste?

Your grandmother's lumpy gravy?

Your aunt's over-cooked turkey?

Let's face it—holidays aren't some independent taste test.

They are our fuzzy golden memories imprinted on our palates.

Anything different than what was, just tastes wrong.

I know in my single years, I was invited to some perfectly lovely holiday dinners. Each time the sweet potatoes stuck in my throat like trying to swallow a boulder.

It wasn't the taste.

It just wasn't my taste.

You don't want to come to our Thanksgiving this year. I'll be serving some concoction of pineapple-less sweet potato blandness that will satisfy those people I now call my family.

Funny thing is, it will probably become my kids' golden taste memory.

Sometime before the end of the month, I'll whip myself up a pan of my mom's sweet potatoes, just like I remember them.

My Thanksgiving gift to myself.

I'll shovel them down as I read your email.

The one where you tell me how you like your sweet potatoes.

Where you share the holiday dish that divides your family.

Your stories will make my "Sweet Potato Party For One" taste all the sweeter.

Daryn@DarynKagan.com.

Do My Fat Thumbs Make Me Look Old?

"That makes you look old," daughter informed me this week, as she watched me do something I do several times a day.

Was she looking at emerging "non-pigmented" roots along my hairline? (I prefer not to use the four-letter word that starts with "g.")

Was I reaching for reading glasses?

Inspecting a new crevice working it's way onto my face.

I do, indeed, have all that fun going on.

This, however, is bigger.

According to my daughter.

More public.

More horrifying.

And something she thinks I can control.

See, the thing is—

I text.

Which is awesome and modern, yes?

But, there's this--

I do it with my single index finger.

Yes, I, who did so well in 7th grade typing class, who can rock a QWERTY keyboard with my eyes closed.

When it comes texting on my phone, I hunt and peck, my right index finger leading the way.

"Why can't you use your two thumbs?" Daughter asks with mild disgust, as she demonstrates thumbs ablaze over the lower third of her phone.

"I didn't know this was an issue," I say in shocked old person shame.

Did you, Dear Reader?

Did you know a teenager can tell your age by how you text, as sure as an arborist can count the rings of an ancient redwood?

I certainly wasn't going to make Daughter the final authority on this or any other issue.

So, I went to the font of truth.

I posted on Facebook.

"Have been informed by certain teen daughter that I text like an old person because I use single index finger instead of double thumb method. What say you?"

"She's right," so many commenters weighed in. "Makes you look old."

So much for Facebook "friends" having my back, or my thumbs, as the case may be.

I would make the argument that it's not a matter of age, rather something I've had since I was much younger.

My whole life, actually.

Fat thumbs.

Make that fat, flat thumbs.

For me to try to get any semblance of a message out using these paddle-shaped digits would create only a jumble of an alphabetic mess that even "Auto-correct" couldn't make sense out of.

It's like trying to talk with 42 saltines shoved in my mouth. You're not going to understand what I'm trying to say and it sure isn't going to be pretty what sprays out.

I'm willing to get out the hair dye bottle.

I'll shuffle around for reading glasses.

Botox? Let's label that, "under consideration."

But double thumbs?

Sorry, just not going to happen.

And Daughter?

Oh, I have big plans for her.

A friend just showed me that microphone icon at the bottom of the screen.

Forget index finger hunt and peck texts.

Here comes my rambling, stream-of-consciousness texts!

Won't be long before she'll be gazing at my index finger feeling nostalgic for, "The good old days."

Y'All--My Family Can't Talk To Each Other

My family needs to talk.

It's not so easy.

"Ah, yes, raising two teenagers," you nod in compassion and understanding.

Yes, thank you.

But that's not it.

Well, it is many days.

The problem, I've diagnosed this week is something bigger.

It starts at the beginning.

We don't speak the same language.

Ours is a family with folks raised in California, the Midwest, and the South.

The basic problem--no one can agree on how to speak. I'm talking simple pronunciation.

There are members of my family who swear the pen you write with and the pin you use to stick something should be pronounced the same.

They'd wager that bet and bit should sound the same.

Let's all sit here awhile until we're all set.

Might as well, since "sit" and "set" are meant to sound the same.

To them, anyway.

I tried a little test, writing three words down on a pad of paper. "Say each word," I instructed my daughter as I revealed each one individually.

"Bin," she said as I showed her the first word, b-i-n.

Next came the boy's name, B-e-n.

"Bin," she said again.

"You say, 'bin' and 'Ben' the same?" I asked, making double-sure.

"Of course," she was already bored with me. "How else would you say it?"

"I say, 'bin' for the container and 'Behn' for the boy's name," I shared.

"No one talks like that," she informed me with great teen authority.

"We can make this even more interesting," I said revealing the third word, b-e-e-n.

"Bin," my daughter said for the third time.

"Let's call your aunt in Canada," I offered, "And ask her."

"Why? How would she say it?"

"Been, same as lima bean," I ventured, thinking of how some Canadian pronunciations have crept into my sister's speech in the seven years she's lived there.

Not that I can point fingers.

When I moved to Atlanta more than 20 years ago to work for CNN, my parents were thrilled for the career opportunity and terrified for what the move could do to my speech patterns.

"The first time you say, 'y'all or 'fixin to,'" my California native parents declared, "we are coming and packing your things. No child of ours will speak like that."

Y'all, they had no idea what was in store or how bad and confusing things would get around here.

It makes for great, shall we say, "debates" at the dinner table where no one agrees that my California speech pattern is accent-free.

Midwestern Husband looks at me like he married a cross between exotic flower and California hippie.

The teens just think the way I talk is simply further evidence of how weird I am.

At least this does explain one mystery of life.

These teenaged girls can't be blamed for not cleaning their rooms.

Poor dears, simply don't understand what I'm saying.

And you, Dear Reader?

Are you living in a house with multiple accents? Spell them out for me at Daryn@DarynKagan.com.

Talk about a potential movie moment gone bust!

The "Woe Is Me" moment was brought on, of all things, by the recent "Sound of Music" Sing-A-Long on TV.

Did you happen to catch it, Dear Reader?

Did you sing along?

As Julie Andrews sings, "Let's start at the very beginning…."

Of coming across the movie on TV, of looking to my family and saying, "Yes, Family let's sing!"

Here's the thing—I didn't get as far as a "deer, a female deer," before my family turned this moment into "So long, farewell, Auf Weidersehen, goodbye!".

Husband declared old, cheesy musicals were not one of his "Favorite Things."

The kids actually suddenly felt inspired to go clean their rooms.

I really shouldn't have been surprised.

My singing is not Something Good.

No, really.

I'm not being humble.

It's bad.

I'm bad.

It's certainly not for lack of enthusiasm.

Perhaps, it's possible you can relate, Dear Reader? Do you have something you love to do, even though you know you have zero talent?

I love to belt out my "Do Re Mi's" with the best of them.

It's just my brain thinks C sharp. And B flat comes squeaking out.

This is not a new challenge for me.

The first clue came when I tried out for choir in sixth grade.

After what I thought was a fine rendition of James Taylor's, "You've Got A Friend," Mrs. Wyatt, the music teacher, looked at me with a stern suggestion, "Have you thought about joining the school newspaper for an elective instead?"

True story--that's how my journalism career was born.

Just as Mother Superior tells Maria, "One door closes and a window opens."

Back to the movie and climbing every mountain. I held my ground on the couch in our den belting out each tune as Julie Andrews and Christopher Plummer fell in love, as the adorable children entertained Austrian aristocracy, as the evil Nazi empire loomed.

My family has no idea what they were missing!

At least my dog stayed with me.

She's loyal.

Well, and at almost 15 years old, totally deaf.

There's that.

Still, I suspect, I'm not alone. Perhaps you have something you love to do, that it turns out you're not particularly good at?

Slowest runner in last weekend's 5k race?

Hack golfer?

Worst baker at that holiday cookie exchange?

Okay, let's be honest—we stink and we love it!

Can we agree to into this new year embracing the joy of it, forget the critics!

You won't have to go it alone.

I can loan you my dog.

At her age, she's slower than you are, still enjoys retrieving a golf ball, (as long as you don't throw it too far,) and she has yet to meet a cookie she doesn't like.

With DarlaDog's encouragement, let's have the gumption to embrace from brings us joy!

Now, everyone, sing along!

Looks like I will be turning in my American passport.

I've been informed I'm not of this country.

And it ratchets up from there.

Apparently, I'm not even of this planet.

The notice came via a look.

A look from my kids.

Perhaps, Dear Reader, you've gotten "The Look," as well?

It comes about the time you mention celebrities or movies that were part of the fabric of your youth.

"This guy reminds me of Elton John," I remarked the other day about a song that came on the radio.

"Ella What?"

"You've never heard of Elton John?" I asked unbelievingly.

"Nope." My kid didn't even feign interest, not a blip of "Tell me more, Mom."

"Who's in the movie?" the other kid asked the other day when I took notice of a new trailer.

"Kevin Costner."

Blank look.

Hottie Kevin Costner! He of "Dances With Wolves," "The Bodyguard" "Bull Durham." "Field of Dreams."

Kevin Costner might be building it, but kids today aren't coming.

Not only do my kids have no clue about the media of my youth, they have no interest in how I consumed it.

"Y'know everything hasn't always been 'On Demand,'" I explained, going to the dark place and time of when you actually had to wait for something you wanted to see.

It's called, wait, big vocabulary word coming, "Anticipation." (Cue the Carly Simon song, just don't bother explaining who she is.)

"If you wanted to watch cartoons you had to get up on Saturday morning."

"What's the big deal?" the kids asked. "We can do that."

"You can watch Saturday morning, Tuesday at lunch, Thursday night," I clarified. "Saturday morning was it for us. Sleep in and Scooby Doo became Scooby Don't."

They put their hands over their ears. "Please stop," they almost begged. The imagery was scarier than watching "The Exorcist" or "Jaws."

My attempts at explaining how a mechanical shark kept me from even going in a swimming pool for an entire summer didn't translate.

The sad thing is I recognized "The Look" because it's the same one I gave my parents when they shared the stories of getting their family's first television set. Or the first time they saw color TV.

That's why there's no need to get too frustrated with my "It's all about now" kids.

I know their day is coming. (Insert revengeful snicker.)

I look at a photo of my daughter. It's just an everyday photo, her arms draped around two of her friends. But there, clutched in her left hand is her cell phone, as it is usually clutched. It's possible it's super glued, even.

I fast-forward about 30 years from now. Her kids will be laughing at her.

"Ewww! Look at that. What is that in your hand?"

"It was called a 'cell phone,'" she'll have to explain. "We used it to watch our favorite shows and text our friends."

Her kids won't hear a word. They'll be too busy giving her "The Look" to launch her to another planet.

Is It Weird I Want A New Best Friend?

I want to ask her to be my new best friend.

I haven't exactly actually met her yet.

There's that.

My teenaged daughter is already freaking out at the idea.

There's that, as well.

"It's stalker, creepy," she informs me.

"What? Dreaming of making someone I've not actually met my new BFF?"

This conversation is over.

There are only so many times she can tell me that anyone over 20 should not be using "BFF."

I can't help myself.

This woman, my hero, has done something so wonderful.

My admiration knows no bounds.

She's been able to do in a single week, something that has stumped my husband and me.

She is my daughter's Economics teacher and she has taught my kid the value of money.

As kids go, we got a good one. Seems to be appreciative and kind.

And as our lives go, I think we've dropped the ball on money. Days move fast, kids have stuff, the value of a dollar seems to get lost in the conversation.

Allowance? Yes? No?

Pay for chores?

Make kids get a job?

All conversations had.

I will not lie. I don't think we've got it right.

Then, along comes 9th Grade "Introduction to Economics."

Ms. Awesome Teacher gave each of the kids a random profession, salary, and family and told them, "Go figure out your life. Make a budget. Buy a house. Feed those kids."

Our daughter was told she is a school principal. We're so proud! How nice to think that college education we're scraping up for will be paying off.

She makes $89,000 a year. She has a husband and three kids. All is not perfect. Of course it's not. Ms. Awesome Teacher knows this is to be a lesson.

Disturbingly, my daughter's pretend husband doesn't contribute financially or take care of these kids. Add childcare to the family budget.

Oh, you know I got my two cents in on her choice in men.

"Your pretend husband is a bum," I informed her. "I don't care how cute he was. There's a reason they call it life 'partner.' You want someone who does their part."

It didn't take long for the fun to begin.

I soon heard the yelling coming from behind her bedroom door.

"Not a chance! No way!"

"What's going on?" I asked with great concern.

"Do you know what cell phones cost?!" she asked with great indignation, as if she was delivering breaking news. "No way are these kids getting unlimited data on their phones!"

"You got to be kidding!" came later cries.

"What's wrong now?" I asked seeing her laptop open to grocery store websites.

"It costs too much to buy all this food for dinner every night."

"Really?" I smiled.

My favorite moment came as she got up from out dinner table later in the week heading back to her bedroom to continue working on her project.

"I'm so sick of making menu plans, budgets, and going to the grocery store," she groaned.

"Welcome to my world, Sweet Daughter. Welcome to my world."

By the time she was done, Sweet Daughter decided that her family would be living an hour away from her job, the free-loader husband wouldn't get a car, and those kids—they could share a room and eat macaroni and cheese for dinner most nights.

"Wow. You're going to be like the world's meanest, cheapest mommy," I teased.

"No, this was just like a reality check," she countered. "Stuff, like, costs a lot of money."

Talk about a million dollar gift!

My kid gets it.

With that, my plans were sealed. Ask Ms. Awesome Teacher to be my new best friend.

And start saving up.

Looks like my future grandchildren have an austere life ahead of them. Someone will need to spoil them. Might as well be me and my husband.

You know--their future BFFs.

We had a crisis in our house this week.

As are most crises with teenagers—

This one was astronomical.

Huge.

Tragic.

It involved,

Get ready.

It's big.

Our daughter losing her cell phone.

Yes, I know.

International relief funds have been started over tragedies smaller than this.

"I think I left it behind at school," she explained in a panic while using someone else's phone. "I couldn't go back and check or I'd miss the bus home."

You can imagine how this crisis set the table for dinner conversation.

"Surely someone stole it," she and my husband believed.

"Maybe a good person picked it up and is holding it for you for tomorrow," I offered.

Multiple eye rolls were my only payment for offering the possibility of well, hope.

As my daughter's stress level continued to rise, I detected teachable moment.

The question is "What do you do with The Wait?

Dear Reader, what do you do with *your* Wait?

That time between now and seeing how something turns out.

Before you get the medical tests back?

Before you find out if you got the job?

Before you know if he will call for a second date?

"I'm going to believe in the good person theory," I told my daughter.

"But, how do you know?" she doubted my optimism.

"I don't," I admitted. "But I also don't know that your phone was stolen. Once you've done everything you can, the only thing you can control is how much time you spend looping the bad possibilities over and over again in your head."

She shrugged her doubting shoulders.

Within the hour of dropping her off at the school bus the next day, I felt my cell phone buzzing in the pocket of my worn sweatpants.

I couldn't help but smile at the caller ID.

My daughter's name was flashing on the screen.

"I got my phone back!" she screamed. "You were right! One of the security guards locked it up for the night. That's why no one answered when I tried to call it or use the tracking app!"

Score one for the good guys.

I can only hope Daughter took note.

Sure, I know the news won't always be good at the end of an anticipated wait.

And I've certainly tortured myself enough times with dreadful "What If's."

You, too?

These days, the "What If's" and I are broken up.

I'm not some evolved spiritual being.

More like a little worn down, broken in.

The journalist in me likes to do an inventory of the facts I actually know. It's usually not much.

There are usually more "What If's" trying to bang around my head than actual facts.

So what if good guys won't always win?

There's plenty of time to deal with muck once I know an actual outcome.

Meanwhile, it sure is nicer to hang out with hope in my head.

That is how I wait.

How about you?

Better to email me at Daryn@DarynKagan.com.

Y'know, just in case I lose my phone.

"Holding my daughter tight with love."

Dear Daughter,

We met when you were 11.

I married Daddy when you were 13.

The judge made you and me legal with our adoption when you were 14.

This parenting gig really does fly by in flash, so before you zoom out the door, on the occasion of your Sweet 16, here are 14 wishes from me to you:

- I wish that you know how much joy you've given your two mothers. Both Mommy in heaven, and now my turn, here on Earth. I know neither of us could ask for a bigger honor than to get to be your mom.

- I wish that you know it's actually not your job to bring joy to anyone. It's okay to use that voice of yours. Speak up. People pleasers often aren't very pleased themselves.
- I wish that you know your girlfriends are some of the biggest treasures you will ever have. They are your sisters by choice. You've picked some awesome ones. Hang on tight with one arm, while welcoming new friends as you travel on.
- I wish that you demand any boy you choose to date treat you with the same love and respect your girlfriends do. This is a high bar. You'll be surprised by how many women settle for less.
- I wish that you remember that you can't screw up the right one; you can't make the wrong one work. This will hold true with relationships, colleges, jobs, and houses.
- I wish that you remember that you're the only one you need to make a party complete. Know that everyone will be exactly where they are supposed to be and you'll never be disappointed with an r.s.v.p. list.
- I wish that you know how you dress matters. Like it or not, you're sending the world a message about you.
- I wish that you know that money matters. No, not to have the most, but to understand it, manage it, and save it will give you enormous freedom.
- I wish that you know that women's intuition is real. Those hairs standing up on the back of your neck, that funny feeling in your stomach— trust them.
- I wish that you know that accomplishments are great, but happiness is a choice.
- I wish you take as much time as you need before you get your driver's license. Daddy and I will sleep better and you get to do life at your own pace.
- I wish you side-blinders so you have no need to look at anyone else's plate. Comparison is a losing game. You'd be surprised how many who appear to have more aren't happy with what they have.

- I wish you appreciation for good health. It's easier to keep than to get back.
- I wish you many mistakes and no regrets. It's called a journey. It's leading you exactly where you need to be. I know because so many of my so-called mistakes, led me to you and Daddy.

Why only 14?

Because 15-16 and all the others are for you to create and go after.

Daddy and I will be here giving you guidance, love and support, but, Hija, this is your ride.

Oh, what a kick to get to watch you launch.

All my love,

Your Madre.

Family

The Man Who Has No Business Loving Me

"With the man we call, 'Pops.'"

He has no business loving me.

The very idea of me could easily inspire a Bitter Party For One.

I wouldn't even blame him.

I am not an answer to his prayers.

And yet...

Here we are at Mother's Day.

I'm the one being celebrated. I'm the one who gets the joy, privilege, and honor of raising his only grandchild.

And yet....

The man we call, "Pops," has experienced more loss than one person should bare: his first wife and both his adult children passing within a few years of each other.

Left behind--only him and his precious young granddaughter.

Twist the knife again as that sweet little girl left his custody after his daughter died and went to live full-time with his former son in-law.

I can only imagine in his pain, his grief, his loss, the last person he was hoping for was me.

After all, who am I?

A California-raised, outgoing, somewhat zany lady who is not of his faith. A faith that is everything to him. A faith that has sustained him through all these tragedies.

And yet...

It is I who showed up three years after his daughter passed.

I, who married his former son in-law.

I, who adopted his granddaughter.

I, who became a mom after his daughter left soon.

How easily he could resent me.

And yet---

Somehow, we work.

Together, we share an endless, over filled heart fueled by love for our girl.

And beyond--

In Pops, I have found a co-conspirator in the cookie jar. I thought I had a naughty sweet tooth. Pops has a sweet tooth that could put Willy Wonka to shame. To dine with Pops means to enjoy the best desserts possible.

From him I've learned the importance of topping just about every sweet with a side of vanilla ice cream. "Knocks the sweetness down a notch," he winks.

In Pops, I've learned to roll with the tide, as in "Roll Tide Roll," as in Alabama Football. As in a passion for a team that runs close behind his love for his God, is beloved second wife, and yes, his granddaughter.

My own sports-loving college football obsessed father must've been smiling down the first time Pops treated me to a home game in Tuscaloosa.

Turns out, my dad passed away the same year as Pops' daughter, my daughter's first mother.

Ironic how things like that happen. In the pain of the moment, you can't see who might be on their way to you.

Wouldn't have mattered if someone told either of us. The story so far-fetched neither would've believed it.

It's not like Pops and I sat down and had a talk one day and agreed, "I'll be compassionate about your loss, if you respect that I've now adopted your granddaughter."

Nope. Never happened.

Somehow, in a potentially stressful, awkward situation where things could've gone terribly wrong, we, two imperfect people, have both managed to show up as our best selves.

I never forget how painful it must be to see another woman raising his daughter's child.

He seems to find any occasion to thank me for being a great mom to his granddaughter.

I'm no replacement for his daughter, as he is no replacement for my dad.

I share this, Dear Reader, to say that I have come to know that amid all the flowers, candy, joy and expressions of unconditional love we mothers are showered with this special day, there is someone out there who is not having the Mother's Day they wished.

It's the thing no one really talks about when families break.

Death.

Divorce.

Shattered Families.

They all have a way of robbing what some deserving soul wishes for this Mother's Day.

If that's you—If Mother's Day is not as you wished this year, know that I'm thinking about you.

Just like I'm thinking about Pops, knowing that he wishes it was his daughter who was here to celebrate. I get it. That's fair.

I also know I'll hear from him wishing me a Happy Mother's Day.

Oh, you know that's going to take my breath away that a man who has lost so much can open his heart one more time for me.

Oh, you know we will be celebrating both my daughter's mothers this Mother's Day.

Oh, you know there will be some awesome dessert.

And oh, yes, indeed we'll knock it down with a side of vanilla ice cream.

These Aunts Got Kids

Do not ask these women if they have kids.

Not if you mean it in the elitist way that some women are greater than others.

As if to suggest women who have birthed a baby out of their body or adopted a human being are better than those who have not.

I'm talking being an aunt.

I'm talking about a particular kind of aunt.

The kind who is not raising some type of human being in their own home.

The New York Times came up with a name for them a couple years ago.

Called them, "PANKs," as in, "Professional Aunt; No Kids."

Marketing executives are apparently anxious to capture the dollars for women who have good jobs, love kids, but have none of their own at home.

Talk about being late to the party.

By the time I knew I was trendy, I wasn't.

I was a PANK for most of my adult life. Until I got married few years ago, I was like a lot of women I know. We certainly never planned on not having children. Our lives just sort of turned out that way, much to the dismay of our kid-loving hearts.

And so, yes, I found great joy in doting on my two nephews and a collection of about a dozen godchildren, both official and unofficial. I used to say, for someone who has no kids, I sure do have a lot of kids. Part of my joy was, indeed, spending some hard earned cash on the apples of my eye. Still, I know *The New York Times* really missed the boat on this one.

It's not about the money you spend on a kid. The role of a devoted aunt is so much more than that.

You are confidante, soother, booster, love infuser, protector, mentor, instigator, inspiration, playmate.

Try putting a dollar value on that, Madison Avenue!

When I got married, I not only got a husband, but a daughter, as well. It had been just the two of them since her mother passed away eight years ago. And so with that simple, "I do," I became a mom, as well. It truly is the deal of a lifetime. It also meant the end of my PANK status, as I now have a kid of my own.

Now, it's I who gets to listen to my daughter wax poetic to her friends about my sister, her new aunt. How fun she is and all the wonderful things they do together. My sister now gets to be the amazing PANK, the co-conspirator in get a second ear piercing. I'm now the mom who has to consider, "Hmmm, I don't know if that's a good idea." (For the record, I lost that one.)

To all the PANKS out there, I just want to say you are so much more than an expensive gift at the holidays.

And the next time someone asks you, "Got kids?"

Make sure you say, "Oh, yes I do!"

You got the luckiest kids in the world.

Lucky, because they have you.

The Birthmark That Wasn't

I wasn't born.

This fact was relayed to me by my slightly older brother. About the time he was six and I was five.

The traumatic childhood memory of this revelation came flooding back to me this week, thanks to an endearing news item I stumbled upon.

I read how two parents in England who got tattoos to match their young daughter's unique birthmark.

Ah, birthmarks.

They run through my family.

I'm talking the port wine stain kind. They are raised, red, obvious marks.

Prime target for getting teased.

My brother has one that looks like splat of cherry jelly running down behind his left ear.

My younger sister was born with a quarter-sized strawberry circle on her left cheek.

And then there was me.

Nothing.

Not a single mark.

You would think this would make me the lucky one.

Not a chance.

My brother saw to that.

Saw a way to turn what could be his negative into his positive.

His tool for doing what older brothers are supposed to do.

Torment younger sisters.

"Well, that just proves it," he casually pointed out to me one day.

"Proves what?" I took the bait.

"Proves you weren't born."

He stated this fact as simply and plainly as the sky was blue.

"I was too born!" I protested.

"Nope. You weren't. That's why they call it a 'birth-mark.' Proof that you were born. No birthmark-no proof-which means you weren't born," he said, quite pleased with himself.

"Mooooooooom!" I went crying to our mother. "Was, was, was I born?"

"Yes, you were born," she assured me.

Since that day, I've tried to take my mother's word over my brother's as to proof of my existence.

Still, a little part of me continued to wish that my birthmark was actually hiding in some corner of my body I hadn't discovered.

You can bet I've looked.

A lot.

Chalk this anxiety up to one of our life long challenges—

Being different.

Kudos to those parents who went the extra mile to assure their beloved daughter she wasn't that different after all.

Truth is, there's only so much a parent can do.

We all feel different in a way.

And as you grow up, the stakes get higher.

What is it for you, Dear Reader?

Feels like you're the only one of your friends who isn't married?

The only one who is struggling financially?

The only one who's kid and is struggling with mental illness?

No reassuring words from Mom or valiant act of tattoo can change that.

Except maybe this.

Maybe the realization that we all get something.

Some get the birthmark.

Some don't.

But we all got something.

Something to deal with.

Something that makes us different.

I'm trying on the idea it's possible being different doesn't have to mean being ashamed.

I'll let you know how that works for me.

That is, as soon as I'm born.

Picking Grandparent Names: The New Baby Boomer Contact Sport?

My cousin is doing well, thank you very much.

She survived a life milestone which I had no idea was supposed to be so challenging.

And yet, as it often is with life passages, things like puberty, parenthood, or gray hair, we learn from those who bravely go before us.

My cousin has picked her grandmother name.

As my mom's first cousin, she's actually kind of late to the grandparent game.

Her older daughter hasn't had kids and her youngest just got started.

There we were connecting at the modern, cyber family reunion, aka, Facebook, "oohing" and "ahhing" over pictures of her new granddaughter when I had to ask, "What's your grandma name?"

"I am Nana," she replied, beaming her new name through the online universe. "Sally, (her mom, my grandmother's sister) was Nanny. The other grandma is Grammy. So Nana was available. Who knew it could be so complicated?"

Complicated indeed.

Apparently, the new baby has two sets of grandparents on her father's side. One of them jumped on the Facebook comment thread, "We're going to let little Olivia decide what to call us."

Was this equally new grandparent suggesting my cousin somehow robbed their mutual granddaughter of some right?

What I took as a jab, my cousin handled with total grace. "Isn't our little one lucky to have so many grandparents," she wrote.

So is this a thing?

Is picking and claiming grandparent names the new contact sport for Baby Boomers?

Both my grandmothers were "Nana."

There was Nana Lil and Nana Ann.

There was no confusing them, as they were two very different women.

My mom is Nana.

Me?

I'm prematurely prepared.

"I already have my grandmother name," I announced last year to my girls. They looked at me with dread.

"I want to be called, 'Guppy!'" I announced with gleeful anticipation of a day that is hopefully many, many years away.

'Guppy' was the girls' first nickname for me as we were becoming a family about five years ago.

Okay, so it came because I had a case of Bells Palsy for a couple of months and my face looked like it was melting off my head. The girls decided I looked like a guppy fish. Maybe not the easiest of times, but Guppy it has been ever since.

"I will be Guppy. And Dad will be Puppy! Guppy and Puppy!"

The kids' expressions looked like I had just served them up a plate of rotten spaghetti.

Who knew there would be an added benefit of this Grandparent name game? I do believe I just came up with a new version of teen birth control. Forget about sex ed, just come up with a horrifying grandparent name. These kids will not be making me a grandmother anytime soon.

That means for now, I need to live vicariously through you, Dear Reader.

Do you have a good story behind your grandparent name? Or the name you call your grandparents?

Share with me at Daryn@DarynKagan.com.

The War-Drobe

10 years later I still can't believe I did this.

I guess when your mother catches you keeping one of the biggest secrets of your life, you do as you're told.

Rewind the tape to 2003, a time when we actually still used videotape, when President George W. Bush had declared the US would invade Iraq. If you remember correctly, he just didn't say exactly when, which, it turns out, set up my predicament.

Over at CNN, where I was a long time news anchor, I was one of those on standby to head to the Middle East as soon as we got the word. I had gone through what they call "War School" safety training. My bags were packed. Everything was crossed off my "To Do" list.

Specifically on my "NOT To Do" list was telling my parents what my plans were.

"Why worry them?" I decided after talking it over with my brother and sister.

Sure, I planned to tell them as I was boarding the plane, but why add the stress of not knowing when I would go?

They certainly had enough on their worry plates. Weeks into the waiting game, I found myself in Los Angeles where my father was in one hospital being treated for internal bleeding and my mother was about to have surgery for her recently diagnosed breast cancer.

That's how my mom and I found ourselves in a hospital cafeteria, making small talk, eating green Jello and bad coleslaw, the night before her surgery.

Somehow, we got talking about the upcoming war. I thought I was so smooth keeping it to politics and generalities. That's when my mother looked me straight in the eye and busted me.

"You're going, aren't you?" she nailed me with that signature look of hers, a look so penetrating, the US wouldn't have needed water boarding to get terrorists to spill. They could've just used my mother's look.

"What do you mean?" I replied digging down for my best denial.

"When the war starts, CNN is sending you to cover it. Aren't they?"

I was more busted than a teenager breaking curfew. I spilled everything.

"Yes, I've been trained. Yes, I'm standing by. No, I didn't tell you. But if you don't want me to go, I won't."

My mother got very quiet. Paused for what seemed like a century.

"What are you going to wear?" she asked.

"Excuse me?" I said.

"What are you going to wear? I mean what are the ladies wearing to war these days? Blazers? Leather jackets? I know! Let's go shopping!"

"Shopping?" I said, not believing her crazy idea. "Dad's upstairs in a hospital bed. You're having breast cancer surgery tomorrow and you want to go shopping?"

"Look," she explained. "I can't control what happens with my surgery. God knows I can't control your father. But, I can control what my kid looks like on international television. You'll do me the greatest favor—if we can just go shopping. We'll call it your 'war-drobe.'"

That's how I ended up in the stores the night before my mother's surgery. Cancer makes you do crazy things. I still have the khaki pants, leather jacket and bright shirts "for a splash of color" we picked out that night.

They were perfect.

It's been 10 years since breast cancer came into our family. 10 years since I reported the start of the war. These days, my life is hardly so glamorous. Jeans and a t shirt cover 99% of my wardrobe requirements as a wife, mother, and columnist.

My mom? 10 years after The War-Drobe, she's still at it.

A large envelope arrived in the mail the other day. Inside was a pretty red dress. It's something I could wear to a fancy dinner party or anchor a newscast.

"Mom, I have nowhere to wear this dress," I protested.

"You'll do me the biggest favor," she said. "You'll keep it. It makes me happy to think you have something in your closet should an opportunity arise."

You know what happened.

I kept the red dress.

Gratitude makes you do crazy things.

10 extra years of having my mom around because doctors caught her breast cancer early.

I'm so glad about that.

And that is no secret.

Best Worst Reason To Get On A Plane

Honeymoon.

Traveling the world as a news correspondent.

Volunteering at an orphanage in Africa.

I've had a lot of great reasons to get on a plane.

I now have the best worst one.

"The doctor called with the test results," my mother said on the phone last week from the other side of the country. "The biopsy shows I have a low-grade form of lymphoma."

The air sucked out of the room and everything on my calendar instantly turned to pencil.

We now face what so many families do—

How do you care for a parent living far away?

"I'm the only one of my friends who doesn't have children living here in town," my mother has pointed out in recent years.

That might be the case for Mom's immediate circle, but I know our family looks like so many others, perhaps ever yours, Dear Reader.

The three of us kids are scattered across the globe having made lives, careers and families far from where we grew up.

None of us has any interest in moving back to our hometown.

And my mother has no interest in leaving it.

The lure of being close to grandchildren and family who could help care for her doesn't come close to staying in the same five-square mile area she has spent her 78 years.

We might not understand each other's choices, but we respect them.

Which leads us to now.

To lymphoma, to a low-grade form of chemotherapy, to something my mom is not looking forward to, especially alone.

And so we kids are doing what we can. Calling in favors to help care for kids, rearrange work schedules, and yes, get on a plane. I took dibs on being there for her first chemo treatment.

"So what do you wear to a first chemo treatment?" I asked. knowing Mom puts a premium on how you dress, no matter what the occasion.

"You're coming all this way? It's going to be so boring," she protested as part of our dance.

"It'll be, what it'll be, but it won't go well if I'm not dressed right."

"In that case," she relented, "jeans, an adorable sweater, and comfy shoes should pull you together."

So, my things are packed. There's a good chance my outfit won't be cute enough.

My stay won't be long enough.

I'll give it my best, just as my brother and sister will do what they can.

My mom will do her best to fight.

I'm leaving on a jet plane.

The first of what will likely be many trips to the West Coast in the coming months.

I can't think of a better worst reason to go.

It Takes A Village To Raise My Mom

It takes a village to raise...

A parent.

You and I have long known about the need of the so-called village of neighbors, friends and family to raise our kids.

Today, I'm thanking the village it takes to care for my mom.

My mom, who has it made it quite clear she's not leaving our hometown where she's spent her entire life, even if all the kids live far away.

My mom, who was diagnosed with a mild form of lymphoma a few months ago and has been undergoing chemotherapy.

Dear Reader, this isn't the column I planned for you this week.

But when I got the call from my brother that, "Mom isn't doing well. You need to get out here." Well, I hit, "Delete" on a lot of plans I had for this week.

So much for the mild form of chemotherapy doctors promised us. Those treatments are kicking her behind.

She's dropping weight faster than a bad dream version of "The Biggest Loser." And she's always been about 100 lbs in soaking wet socks, so she doesn't have any weight to spare.

So, how did I do it?

Drop everything to go?

I could only pull it off thanks to The Village.

My brother who was the first responder, driving hundreds of miles when he didn't like how our mom sounded on the phone.

My sister who will pick up next week when I have to leave.

My aunt and uncle who live in the same town.

My mom's friends who pitch in how they can even though they are all pushing 80 and have physical ailments of their own.

On the home front, I marvel at my husband who is able to pull out frequent flyer plane tickets like a magician's rabbit popping out of a hat. How he doesn't blink at going into "Single Dad" mode.

Our kids who are taking care of our menagerie of pets.

The neighbors and fellow parents who said, "Sure, no problem," when I ask can you help with school pick up, a ride to the airport.

I could go on and on and I know you would understand. Chances are you have your own village helping to take care of your parents.

I bet you could even be part of someone else's village.

That was me, just last week when my friend's dad suffered a stroke. "What's one more?" I insisted as I picked up her daughter and adopted her for a few days.

I sure like being part of someone else's village better than having to ask for help.

To all my people who have said, "Yes."

To you, who are a part of your friend's village.

Let me just say, "Thank you."

I couldn't be here taking care of my mom without you.

Sometimes, Death Helps

My dad and I are getting along much better these days.

Which is interesting, especially considering he has been gone for more than six years now.

Gone, in the sense of he passed away.

Gone, in the sense of it was his time.

Gone, in the sense that what's left of him, here in my heart, finally feels good.

The enormity of the positive and negative influence my father had on me was twisted together like a mighty tornado zooming across the countryside.

There was Dream Dad who made our lunches, attended every sporting event, spoiled us, showed us the country.

Dream Dad, who was present for us kids and so many of our friends at a time when a lot of divorced dads were not.

And there was Twisted Dad, making questionable choices financially, not understanding proper physical and emotional boundaries.

"Who are you to say what's appropriate?" he would question when I would complain I didn't feel comfortable with some of his words and actions.

Dear Reader, have you had to make sense of a love that did so much good and harm at the same time?

From here, I can see it is not an accident it took me until 49 to get married for the first time. There was a lot of unraveling to do of good and bad before I was ready to pick a good husband.

The death of someone you love can be horrifying, heart ripping, knock you to your knees, causing earth-shattering pain.

It can.

And, then there is the thing that really no one dares to say, at least, never did to me.

So, I will to you.

Sometimes, death helps.

These days, I smile when I rip out a hole in a piece of bread to make a "Cowboy Egg" for my daughter, just like my dad used to make for me.

I laughed while talking to my Dad during the Final Four basketball tournament, as we always used to fill out brackets together. Those twin brothers, Aaron and Andrew Harrison on the Kentucky team would have fascinated him.

"Always thought I'd have twin sons starring on a sports team," he used to say.

The twins never came along, but three of us kids did, each one with a twisted, difficult relationship with him.

From where he is now, I know he's proud of each of us when we pick ourselves up after each of our failures.

"Walk it off," he'd command no matter the wound physical or emotional demanding of us the very thing he was not able to do himself.

In death, I don't have to worry about his making terrible choices, about feeling responsible for cleaning up his messes.

In death, I can just enjoy him.

In death, I can appreciate that he had a pretty warped childhood and rose up the best he could. Doesn't forgive many of his choices, but explains them.

So why share now? Good question.

It's not his birthday or Father's Day. Something just told me that a Dear Reader needed to hear this week, that yeah, sometimes death helps.

Truth is, except for an occasional serial killer, no one is completely bad or completely good.

Truth is, sometimes leaving is the biggest gift the person you love can give you.

My dad's passing has felt like that for me.

It helps me love him more than ever.

Girlfriends

Friendship Is Like A Stack of Pancakes

My friend called this week to explain something I'd never considered.

Great friendship comes down to a stack of pancakes.

Her sweet call was apparently prompted by a visit with another friend of hers.

A friend who has just filed for divorce.

"Being there for her reminded me how you were there for me," my friend said in a voicemail that I know I will keep for a long time. "How years ago you were there for me during my divorce, how every Saturday for at least nine months you faithfully came out to breakfast with me. By my count, that's 36 pancakes. 36 pancakes that got me through a dark time. I just want to thank you again for everyone of those pancakes."

This is where our versions of the same story diverge.

Sure, I remember those Saturday morning breakfasts.

Fluffy buttermilk pancakes, melting butter oozing down the sides, a pool of maple syrup for dipping, as I'm a pancake dipper, not drencher.

I remember looking forward with great anticipation to that Saturday morning date, as well.

It's just that I remember the story as my friend getting me through a tough time, not the other way around.

I remember being new in a town and recently dumped by a long-term boyfriend who I had thought was The One.

Yeah, you remember him. You had one of those, too?

I remember it like this: I knew very few people in town. But, at least every Saturday morning, there would be my friend's laugh, her honesty, her friendship. And someone else's tears.

Yes, some weeks, those could be some salty pancakes.

There's also the small matter that my math for this story works out differently.

Truly, I think my friend remembers a Jenny Craig version.

36 pancakes?

One pancake per week?

That doesn't compute with my "He dumped me who cares if I gain 10 lbs?" memory of the story.

Oh no, there was at least a short stack of pancakes served up each of those Saturdays.

At least.

Which makes mine a 108-pancake memory.

I do believe I still have those fat jeans stuffed in the back of my closet to prove my point.

The important thing is, my friend proved hers.

That even though, all these years later, living 500 miles apart, both happily married to better men than those who broke are hearts, you never forget a true friend.

A real friend.

The kind my friend will now be to her girlfriend who is facing her challenges.

"We're going to be eating a lot of pancakes," she said as she wrapped up her voicemail. "And I just wanted you to know you'll be sitting with us at that counter in spirit for every single bite."

So, Dear Reader, this column is for you.

You, who has had a friend there for pancakes. Who can't remember who was really helping whom through a dark time.

Thank God, for you.

For our friends.

For pancakes.

Now, would someone please pass the syrup?

I'm Getting A New Set of Boobs Tomorrow

I'm getting a new set of boobs tomorrow.

Uh oh. Have you just stepped into a classic case of over sharing?

In a word, yes.

This boob journey is one I never wanted to share. Didn't want to share it with you. Really didn't want to share it with the woman I consider my best friend.

See, the boobs in question are not exactly mine.

They're hers.

That phone call seven months ago where she said, "The biopsy came back positive this time. I have breast cancer." I didn't want to share that with her either.

But share is what you do when you have this kind of friend. That true, real, love you for who you are, not who and what they think you should be, family by choice, kind of friend.

We make so much of wanting the husband, the kid, the job, the riches. We forget one of the greatest journeys we'll ever take is simply as a friend.

If you have at least one, it only takes one, great friend in your life, you're blessed. If you have more than one, well, you've cashed in on one of life's great lottery prizes.

It also means you know The Phone Call.

So, it might not have been the "I have cancer" Call. Maybe it was, "I found out he was cheating and my heart is shattered in a thousand pieces," Call.

Or the "I got laid off…again," Call.

Or the "I'm so embarrassed and mortified to say what my kid did today. How do you do this parenting thing?" Call.

The point is, if you have that one friend, who you would die for, who you feel has saved your life, you've taken that call. Good chance you've made the call, too.

True friendship is raw, naked, real, golden and glorious.

My friend and I have laughed harder than the top button of our jeans could hold in. We've cried so hard over sad, challenging times that bodily fluids have come out of places we didn't know possible.

What happens to her happens, to happens to me.

And so, when I got that phone call, it wasn't my best friend who had breast cancer. WE got breast cancer. That awful, overly cocky, uninvited plague inserting itself into our lives.

We've spent seven months alternating some of those ugly, juicy cries with fighting back. Surgery, pathology, treatment plans, drugs. We've batted each one down like super heroes taking down villain after villain.

My friend is the real hero, here, of course. It's her body and our fight. She's Batman. I'm just one of her many Robins watching her back, taking the flank, letting her know she's not alone for all the parts of this journey she never would've picked, which by the way, includes new boobs.

Though never, shall we say, greatly endowed, my friend is the last woman in the world who would've signed up to enhance what nature gave her. But, as long as you're asking, "What kind of boobs would you pick if you could?" sure has made for some interesting conversations. Who knew that you could consider life, relationships, sex, exercise, fashion, body image, parenting, geometry, gravity and new bras simply by talking boobs?

I think we've got it down. If not, we'll abide by the truth of most of life's big decisions—it's not a tattoo. We'll talk about getting a new set.

We'd prefer to move onto other topics, but we'll do what we have to.

It's what I do for my friend, what she would do for me and I know you do for yours, too.

So, see, it's not just a boob job happening tomorrow. It's a friend job. Getting to fulfill that is one of the greatest honors of my life.

And that's worth sharing any day.

The Night Cancer Didn't Get To Win

Too many days.

Too many days, that awful, despicable, rude, ruthless bully called, "cancer" has knocked on the door of those I love.

That day in high school when it took the life of my best friend, Cyndi's, mother.

That day just out of college when my roommate, Sandra's, mother was diagnosed. Doctors gave her less than a year. She got the rare last laugh and lived 10 more.

That day in '97 when it was my other roommate, Heidi's mother who was diagnosed.

In 2003, it was my own mother.

And just last year, as I shared with you here, Dear Reader, it was Heidi, herself.

Diagnosed with breast cancer.

Cancer won each of those days.

Gave us moments we thought we were defeated.

Then, there was last week.

Last week, hosted the night cancer didn't get to win.

That night.

That one night something so special happened.

Sandra and Heidi, my dear friends, my college roommates had their bat mitzvah.

Yes, you got that right.

Bat Mitzvah.

As in the ritual that Jewish girls have to enter adulthood when they 13 years old.

Only, when Heidi and Sandra were growing up, they didn't have that opportunity.

So, they decided to do it, well, now.

Together.

I flew out to California for a service and the night I knew I would not miss.

My date? Of course, it was Cyndi.

Cyndi, who lost her mom to cancer.

Cyndi, who has shared every milestone with me since that first day of kindergarten. Sitting side by side that night in the synagogue pews, Cyndi and I smiled looking up at Heidi and Sandra having their sacred moment.

We smiled this night because we knew this was the night that cancer could not win.

We smiled because we knew there is not a single person who chooses cancer, but here were Heidi and Sandra showing us that you still do get to choose.

No matter what your faith.

You get to choose to do what's important.

You get to show, that sometimes, it's not too late to do what many might've done decades before.

You get to choose the bond of lifelong friendships, of being there for the darkest and happiest of times.

When it came to the part of the service where the rabbi asks, "Is there anyone who has a loved one who is ill who needs our prayers?" Cyndi stood up.

"Who are you praying for?" the rabbi asked in front of the entire synagogue.

"My younger sister, Jennifer," she shared as the tears began to flow.

See, just last month, cancer came knocking again. This time it's Jen, who is fighting breast cancer.

As Cyndi sat back down, we prayed, we cried, we hugged.

Holding onto each other.

Holding onto hope for Jen's recovery.

Protecting against all the days that cancer tries to take away.

Holding onto the knowledge that cancer can never take away that night, or our friendship, or our commitment to each other.

On that front, cancer will never win.

Serving Hope On Christmas China

Sometimes you just can't fake happy.

You've suffered a loss that's just too big.

A friend reminded me of that this week.

Got me thinking back to a time a few years back when my best lady friends were gathered around a dining room table celebrating my birthday.

As often happens, we each went around sharing updates on our lives.

"Taking a trip to France this summer," Tricia beamed.

"New job is going great," Kim shared.

Yeah, we're a pretty upbeat bunch.

Admittedly, all the "up" can be a bit much.

Which leads me to Betsy and her turn.

"I'm bitter!" she announced bringing our positivity to an abrupt halt.

In truth, I think she scowled, "I'm #%(#$ bitter!" But I'll clean the story up for purposes of sharing in this family newspaper.

"Henry got the Christmas China."

"Henry," we knew was Betsy's soon-to-be ex-husband. The cheating spouse who managed to break her heart and finances.

Talk about talent.

"The house, the 401K, the boat," I was willing to let all of it go," she shared. "But the Christmas China? The #(#*%* Christmas China? I loved those dishes!"

I had to go look up, "Spode Christmas China" to appreciate the beauty of the white plates with Christmas trees on the front. Apparently, this is a big thing to a lot of folks come holiday time. Certainly, was to Betsy.

Fast forward a few months, my friend, Dana, who was also at that party, but knows Betsy only casually through me, got a call from her mother who was working her way around an antique store in a small Tennessee town.

"Dana," she said in her Southern drawl, "They have the most beautiful set of Spode Christmas China for a really great price. I thought you might like a set."

Dana's heart lit up like a Christmas tree.

"Whatever you do, buy that China right away!" Dana told her mother.

It was April by the time that China made its way from Tennessee to Dana to Betsy.

First thing she did was set out the plates on the wobbly table in her small apartment.

"These are the most beautiful dishes I've ever seen," Betsy squealed. "The pattern is even prettier than the dishes I lost and this set has more pieces!"

Don't you know those dishes sat out on Betsy's table for that entire year.

"Because I can," she exhaled.

I believe they were the first ray of sunshine in one of the darkest chapters of Betsy's life. When she had to rebuild her life, her heart, her finances, her home.

I shared the story of the Christmas China the other day with a friend who is suffering a new loss.

She can't fake happy right now.

But she loved Betsy's story.

Betsy, who is now married to an awesome guy.

We raised a toast to friends who give us a moment to be bitter.

Who call in small miracles to help us fill in our empty spaces.

To hope.

And of course, to Christmas China.

When Divorce Means Losing Your Friend's Spouse

I got a divorce this week.

Thank goodness, no.

Not my husband and I.

I think he would agree that were going pretty darned strong as we cross into our third year of marriage.

Still, I got a divorce.

A friend of mine let me know she and her husband made their split official.

Signed the papers.

Done.

Over.

And so I mean I got a divorce, Dear Reader, in the way I know you have, too.

In that divorce doesn't just happen to the two people ending their marriage.

It happens to everyone in the couple's world.

Everyone who loves them.

And, I do love this couple.

I can't and won't lie.

I wouldn't say that about all my friends' husbands.

You know how "The Friend's Husband Standard" goes—he makes her happy and I get my own time with her. That's about all I ask.

But every once in awhile a friend hits it out of the park.

Such was this case.

This was a husband I liked.

I liked them together.

And, I loved their story.

When we gathered seven years ago to celebrate their marriage, there was such a joyous sense of, "Of course! That's why it had taken these two so long to find love, because they were destined for each other all along."

There was a sense that love stories do come true, long before I could see my own unfolding.

In fact, I joked that the toaster that still sits on my kitchen counter was my first wedding present.

This couple received two identical toasters as wedding presents, so I bought one off of them.

Boom. My first wedding present.

Just like I don't know exactly what happens inside my fancy toaster, none of us really knows what's really cooking in someone else's relationship.

So, perhaps, this divorce is for the best.

It's not for me to say.

What is for me to say is the divorce is not theirs alone.

No divorce is.

Not if there are kids, which, it turns out in this case, there are not.

Not if you liked the guy.

Not if you liked them together.

You don't get to ask me to love your person and then expect me to unlove them just because you guys can't make the marriage thing work.

I share this divorce news with you, Dear Reader, because I know you've gotten one, too.

You've felt the loss.

Maybe the loss of your son-in-law who you like better than your own daughter.

Maybe the loss of a good friend.

Maybe just the loss of what was a good love story.

What to do with that?

I'm choosing to celebrate the love that was.

Maybe it wasn't meant to be here forever.

But it was here once.

I'm holding onto that as hope that my friend can find that again.

That they both can.

I'll let go their marriage.

But I won't let go love for both of them.

I won't let go hope.

Forbes Magazine Has No Idea What A Powerful Woman Is

Is it possible to be rude, bored and fired up all at the same time?

I'm thinking, "You, bet!" as I look the latest "25 Most Powerful Women" list from *Forbes Magazine*.

Rude, in the sense that I'm ready to tell this highly respected business magazine what I think of their list. And I'm not thinking "Yeah, Baby! You hit it!"

Bored, as in the sense, that I have time to do such web surfing because I'm stuck at home in one of those dreaded six-hour windows waiting for the air conditioning fix-it person.

I'm even more bored with this so-called powerful women list. It's really it's a collection of the same ol' same ol'.

Prime ministers, media types, CEO's, high tech gurus, and celebrities.

Don't get me wrong: I'm all for women making strides in the workplace.

For progress.

For opportunity.

There was even a time, in an earlier chapter of my life when I would've gobbled this kind of list up with great envy, daydreaming of a time, perhaps, when I might make such a list.

Now?

Now, the list itself emits from me a whimper of an "Eh."

What is it?

Age? Motherhood? Having the opportunity to survive my share of bumps in my road? Maybe all of that and more, which makes me think of powerful women in a whole different way.

And that, Dear Reader, is where I get *inspired*.

I imagine myself invited to address the Forbes editors who come up with such a list.

Powerful?

Powerful, I would explain to them, is my friend, Melissa, who went to the doctor a few months ago thinking she had pneumonia, only to find out she's facing Stage 4 Ovarian Cancer. Powerful, is watching this Steel Magnolia fight back with a smile on her face and a determination not to be fooled with.

Frankly, if I was cancer, I'd be afraid.

Very afraid.

Powerful is Melissa's mother, Gloria, who is right there by her only child's side. And when she's not, it's because she's caring for her husband who has Alzheimer's.

How do caregivers like Ms. Gloria get up to face each day? This is the kind of power that now leaves me in awe.

Powerful is my sister-in-law, Sara who powers through life with Crohn's Disease, not knowing when this awful disease will choose to upend her intestines and her life with wrenching pain.

Powerful is my sister, Kallan, Sara's wife, who has dedicated her life to her love for more than a decade. When Sara hurts, Kallan hurts.

Powerful is my friend, Kate Fletcher, who channeled her grief of losing her husband into creating a home for orphaned girls in Kenya.

Hey, Forbes—powerful is my neighbor, D'lynne, who just delivered a healthy nine pound baby boy.

I'm the stalker neighbor who invites herself over a few too many times, just to have a chance to hold this miracle. And as I do, I marvel at how in the world did D'lynne know how to make a kidney, an eyelash, a brain, for heaven's sake!

Dear Reader, something tells me you know the kind of powerful woman I'm now fascinated with.

I imagine, there's even a good chance it's you.

You, who also gave birth to a wonderful baby.

You, who are raising a child with special needs.

You, who held your parent's hand until their final breath.

You, who picked yourself up off the floor after that gut-wrenching death or break up.

You are among those who make up my "Most Powerful Women" list.

I am also holding a space for the powerful woman to come.

As I'm still sitting around waiting for that air conditioning repair man to get here, I look forward to the woman, and oh, you know it will be a woman, who creates the system where service providers can give you a specific time they will at your house.

That woman will make a billion dollars. She will deserve every penny and she will no doubt make the very top of my most powerful woman list.

Dear Reader, I'd love to know who makes up your "Most Powerful Woman List."

Let me know at Daryn@DarynKagan.com.

"How do you pick your friends?"

What an awesome question I was thrilled to get recently from a certain young person in my life.

Let's talk "The Picker."

The one that selects the friends you choose to have in your life.

My own Picker has been shaped and modified for the better by three wonderful friends over the years.

Thank you, Gina, for explaining it all boils down to fruit.

"Picking good friends is like walking through the produce aisles at the grocery store," she told me. "There's plenty that looks good at first glance, but you have to pick up each piece. Does it feel right? Smell good? Seem like it is a good thing to put in your body? Will they nourish you? Or bring you pain? There will be some friends that seem like a good choice at first, but upon closer inspection, you find they should be put back on the shelf and left behind."

Thank you, Tricia, for teaching me that those good friends are the baseline for picking a good man.

"What kind of girlfriends do you have?" she once asked me.

"The best!" I declared, thinking the sweetest cherries and berries. Not a mushy apple in the bunch.

"Perfect. Now, you should expect the same standards in a romantic relationship that you get from your girlfriends," she spelled out.

This might sound like, "Obvious 101" to you, Dear Reader.

Me?

It was a big clonk over the head.

One that I wasn't ready to hear until my 40's.

I looked at the magnificent group of women friends who surrounded me and enriched my life. Then, I looked at the stupidly long list of junk I'd accepted from various men over the years. Things I wouldn't have stuck around for with a female friend.

Not

A

Chance.

That rotten fruit would've been back on the shelf faster than you could say, "Squished banana."

That one nugget changed my focus on the kind of man I was looking for.

Don't give me too much credit.

It took Sandra to put on the final polish.

"You want to pick a 'Hand Over Heart,' kind of guy," she counseled me after a big break up she was not-so-secretly happy to see come to pass.

"Hand over heart?"

"Yes," she said. "The kind man who would lay down his life for you, who is such a good solid person that you find yourself actually putting your hand over your heart when you describe him."

You can bet that Gina, Tricia, and Sandra were all there a couple of years ago when I married my Mr. SummerFest.

I caught a glimpse of Sandra as I walked down the aisle.

Yep, she had her hand over her heart.

"Good pickin', my friend," she said.

Talk about the ultimate fruit salad kind of day.

The Birthday Wish List

"Have you made your birthday wish list yet?"

It was one of my girlfriends on the phone with the annual prompting that comes long before the calendar reminds me—my birthday is on the way.

I imagine for many women that brings with it depression over what you haven't accomplished, the additional lines that rudely took an uninvited residence on your face this past year and plans to just ignore the day all together.

I don't have that luxury.

No room or time for that around here.

Not with the Pretty Ladies leading the way.

As I've mentioned before, the Pretty Ladies are my amazing women folk. We call ourselves "The Pretty Ladies," well, because we enjoy the pretty. Membership is more a state of mind than anything official, yet it does have some challenging demands, especially around birthday time.

As her special day approaches, each Pretty Lady is expected to say how she wants to be celebrated and create her "Birthday Wish List." The List can include anything, though they tend to be a combination of stuff, moments you'd like to create in the next year, and personal and professional goals.

It felt like mine was coming rather easily this year. I believe white birthday cake with white icing you get at the supermarket is one of God's finest creations. So, we'll have plenty of that. I thought of some "stuff" like a new flat screen TV and new dishes would be nice. I also wrote down a family trip celebrating my upcoming Mom's 75th birthday. And if my beau, "Mr. SummerFest," wants to whisk me off to a getaway sometime soon—Uh, Babe- -my things are packed.

All that came easily, and yet something was missing. Couldn't put my finger on it so I called Kate Atwood. She's one of the younger, hipper Ladies, who really knows how to get creative. She's a young woman who was only 12 when she lost her mom to breast cancer. That sad little girl grew up to create Kate's Club, an organization for kids who have lost a parent or sibling. She's all about creating different, positive experiences, even from tragedy.

Not that my birthday was tragic, but I did need some help. "Working on the birthday wish list," I told her. "Any ideas?"

"Have you thought about giving it away?" she threw out there.

"Giving it away?" I asked. Talk about throwing the car into reverse. "I thought birthdays were about getting."

"Oh, you'll get," Kate assured me. "You'll get double the joy when you use your birthday to raise money for a favorite cause. We'll still celebrate and gift you, but wait until you see how much joy you get out of making an impact."

Kate told me about a website called FirstGiving.com that makes it all really easy. five minutes later, my personal page was up and I was in the business of giving my birthday away.

I picked Hekima Place, a home for orphaned girls just outside of Nairobi, Kenya. It was started by another favorite Kate of mine, American Kate Fletcher, a woman well into her 70's who shows me constantly that it's never too late to give back.

I visited Hekima Place at the end of 2008 and fell in love with the girls, the staff and the purpose—giving a loving family and education to girls who have lost parents to HIV/AIDS.

For my big birthday giveaway, I'm suggesting donations that are any multiple of 26, the day of the month my birthday falls on.

Talk about fun! Who has time to be bummed about a birthday when I'm busy daydreaming about all the good my special day will inspire? Clothes, medicine, and books for the girls in Kenya? It's even better than thinking about the possibility of pretty new dishes or a new TV! Who would want to skip that kind of opportunity? Bring on the birthday!

The Pretty Ladies are gathering for brunch on Sunday. Sounds like Mr. SummerFest has something up his sleeve. And I checked—plenty of cake in the supermarket's bakery section.

Something tells me you or someone you know has a birthday coming up this year. To quote Kate Atwood, "Have you thought about giving it away?" I highly recommend it. What better use of your birthday wish than making someone else's dreams come true?

Salty Goodbyes

Here's hoping the ladies won't mind some extra salty seasoning in the appetizers this weekend, as we gather to wish one of my favorite people in the world, "Goodbye."

For years, my friend, Lori, and her husband have had this crazy dream---once their youngest child was out of high school they were up and moving to live full time in their cabin in Montana. No sooner was their daughter's diploma in hand, when that moving van was pulling up to their front door.

I happen to belong to a magnificent group of ladies who like to gather be it for birthdays, showers, and like now, goodbyes. Seems like every time we get together, I get a request to make a specific appetizer, my "Cowboy Caviar."

It's a crazy combination of black-eyed peas, corn, tomatoes, cilantro, green onions and avocado. I can't tell you exactly why this unexpected combination of flavors works, but it's a hit every time.

In that way, I guess friendship is like cowboy caviar. Are your friends like this, too? Not a lot of people would put you all together, but for some reason, together, you make a delicious combination.

Our Lori is so sweet, wise, and carries her love right at the surface. She's always the first to cry for reasons happy and sometimes sad. She is part of our tight knit group who have met up each weekend for a long run. Those miles have been like therapy sessions jogging our way through broken hearts, lost jobs, and challenging children. And they have been playtime. We wear fuzzy bunny ears on Easter weekend. Lori egged me on to wear a rhinestone tiara for the run on the day of my wedding. And she's been known to carry a pom pom or two to celebrate birthdays and big accomplishments.

I know I should be happy for such a good friend and wonderful person to have her dream come true.

I am, but between you and me-- a big part of me is faking it.

Letting go is simply the ingredient I find hardest to toss in with those that I love.

It's like sending a kid off to college, leaving the boyfriend you love but know you'll never make each other happy long term. And now sending a beloved friend off on her dream come true. I grasp for a dash of the old Richard Bach saying, "If you love someone, set them free."

I also know it has often been me that other friends have wished well as I've gone for my big dreams.

And so I will chop up the tomatoes, onions, corn and cilantro for this weekend's party. You'll know the truth---that I'll be crying as I chop. The ladies might guess when they taste that extra salt.

I will gather myself up and walk into that Goodbye party with a smile on my face.

It's what Lori deserves.

The rest of that quote...

"If you love someone, set them free. If they come back they're yours; if they don't they never were."

She'll be back. For business trips. For visits, for occasional weekend runs.

If all else fails. Lori's already invited us to a gathering at her cabin next September.

I'm so there.

And yes, I'll bring the Cowboy Caviar.

My Husband Wants Me To Start Dating

My husband wants me to start dating.

Wait, it gets better.

He wants me to start dating women.

If this isn't among his sweetest, most endearing qualities, I don't know what is.

See, we're not that wild, exciting swinging couple you might be imagining.

About as far from that as possible.

Look "boring" up in the dictionary and there are our contented, smiling faces.

The deal is, Husband is worried about one of the greatest treasures of my life: my girlfriends.

Let me tell you, I have some amazing friends.

What I lacked for in a husband and kids all those years of being single, I certainly made up for in friends.

The local gang is unofficially known as, "The Pretty Ladies," simply because we enjoy the pretty.

Truth is, when we first started dating, Husband didn't get all the Pretty Lady gatherings-birthdays, holidays, just because, and more.

"You meet your friends *every* Sunday morning to go for a run?"

"Yeah, it's the greatest," I smiled. "We run, we talk, and have coffee. It's like our weekly golf game," I said trying to talk in guy terms.

Thing is, as a single dad raising his daughter alone, my husband didn't have time for things like golf. And I think he was kind of jealous of my time with my friends.

But a couple years into marriage. He gets it. Boy, does he get it.

How my girlfriends energize and motivate me.

How they make me happy.

How they fill up an entirely different part of my heart than the huge chamber that's reserved for him.

Husband is freaking out because two of my best friends, my running Pretty Ladies, are moving on.

One moved to Montana.

One is getting ready to move to the beach full time.

What do you do, Dear Reader, when your girlfriends move away?

If you're me, you're sad and trust that another great Pretty Lady is on her way to fill the void.

If you're Husband, you freak out.

"We need to get you some new Pretty Ladies!" he declares on a daily basis.

And he's looking everywhere.

I come back from an exercise class.

"Wow, that was a good workout," I share.

"More importantly, did you see any potential new Pretty Ladies?" he asks desperate.

No matter where I go, the grocery store, walking the dog, carpool line, "Meet any PL candidates?" he wants to know.

I'm not worried because of all things I'm not good at, making friends is not one of them.

I keep my friends, too.

Still have that same bestie from the first day of kindergarten.

Weekly, Sunday runs might not be the same, but we'll run together when they come to visit.

I might try out coffee with some new friends or fit in an extra girls' trip this year, just to stretch my Pretty Lady wings.

Whatever it takes to make Husband happy.

Losing My Job And Other Stuff That's Hard

"Before one of the biggest changes of my life, anchoring the news at CNN."

"Political correspondent Jeff Greenfield leaving CBS News!" the headlines blared on the TV news insider blogs.

This week also brought me news of a CNN executive leaving her job after 24 years.

I also see on Facebook that a "friend," distant acquaintance, really, who was a senior corporate vice president is out looking for work.

Another friend faces a high profile divorce.

Two things always happen to me when I see someone facing big loss.

First, I get a pang in my gut. I know what it feels like to lose so much. I ended a relationship with someone I loved very much and found out CNN wouldn't be renewing my contract all within two weeks of each other. Gotta say, that wasn't the most fun time of my life. It felt like the biggest things I called myself instantly went away.

Like someone took a wrecking ball to what was my life.

I know what it is to feel loss.

To lose.

To feel like a loser.

Now my confession:

After the empathetic pang for those facing loss, I smile.

Yes, smile.

I know it's possible, if you seize the invitation to grow and really "get it," losing makes everything going forward so much richer.

You get to see that we really are not any these titles we love to cloak ourselves in.

Fancy job title, someone's spouse, even someone's parent.

It's easier to see that once they go.

You're still here.

The title is not.

I also smile because I know that losing something or someone you cherish makes room for new things and titles to come in.

Things you'd never imagine.

Like love.

My beau, Mr. SummerFest, showed up after that wrecking ball cleared my heart and my life.

We were recently on vacation with his daughter and family when I overheard the kids talking about me. "She writes books," they explained to one of the cousins. "And she writes a newspaper column, but not the comics or the action stuff," they summed up.

Pretty good summation from the mouths of babes. I might need to borrow that, as I try to figure out how I fit all that on my business card.

Here comes one of those smiles again.

I know without the CNN chapter and earlier relationship going away, there wouldn't have been room for this professional chapter, or even more importantly, this family chapter.

So, yeah, I smile for you, even while you're losing something big.

Go ahead and have your "sad."

It's really important to feel the feel.

I certainly felt mine.

Deeply.

For months.

Here's what I know—

Your deck just cleared.

For a new job.

A new title.

New love.

New possibilities.

These new ones will be even sweeter than what and who has left.

This time you'll know that nothing lasts forever.

Everything has a beginning, middle and an end.

Yes, everything ends.

You'll get to appreciate wonderful jobs and loving people while they are here, as the gifts that they are, rather than as things that define you.

It is why I will be sending an email to Jeff Greenfield and my other friends facing transitions.

Each time the subject line reads, "Congratulations! "

Maybe this could even be an email to you or someone you know.

I wish they had something like this on Evite.

What if it's possible that loss isn't the end of your world?

That it might be an invitation.

An invitation to grow.

An invitation to a new title.

For as long as it lasts.

Just imagine if you rsvp'ed, "Yes!" to that.

Change Comes

"Did you ever see it coming?"

A lot of folks ask me that about losing my anchor job at CNN.

For the longest time, my immediate response was, "Not at all."

But as time has passed, as the next chapter of my life has taken shape, I can look back on that time like an archeologist digs through a disaster site.

I see a very different story.

Turns out, I was getting ready all along.

I just didn't know it.

On the outside, my life was like the shiny candy coating on the outside of an M&M. In my 12-year career at CNN I covered some of the most important events of that time. Perhaps you were watching on 9/11 as I reported the second plane crashing into the World Trade Center Tower. Or you saw me report live from Kuwait during the start of the war or travel to Africa with Bono or even get all dolled up and go live from Oscar's red carpet.

There's no doubt about it — being a CNN news anchor is an amazing job. I loved it on the outside.

On the inside, there was more struggle.

Now, I can see that there were clear signs that change needed to happen, was already happening, long before I realized.

I came back from covering the war convinced that risking my life for the big story would make the network fall in love with me and give me a huge promotion.

My bosses fell in love, alright.

With a new anchorette who had been at the network just a few months, safely ensconced in the Atlanta newsroom while I was halfway around the world dodging Saddam Hussein's missiles.

My old job was waiting for me and the bosses made sure I understood I was lucky to have it.

I also thought going through war with my then current beau would cement our relationship.

Yeah, he came back and married an old girlfriend.

It was definitely a hit your forehead into a brick wall moment. "What's the point of all that I do if it doesn't bring the results that I want?" I wailed to my pity party self.

It was a miserable time of my life.

Ah, yes.

Misery.

What a gift it can be.

It opened me up.

Misery opened me to a new way of thinking.

Misery opened me to what started as a toe-dipping spiritual journey that has grown into a full relationship with God.

I figured out that it's not what I *do* that has the power.

It's who do I choose to *be*.

Talk about reshuffling all the pieces of the jigsaw puzzle of life.

I could get up each day, deciding to focus on positive things happening in my life and what I could do for others, rather than waiting for them to do for me.

It's almost like child's play when you first try it, like holding a Star Wars laser.

This is powerful stuff.

Since I was assigned to a non-prime time show, I had flexibility in what we put in the newscast. I created a segment called, "Your Spirit," stories about people who were doing positive things in the world. I loved doing those stories, even though I had to shoot and wrote them on my own time.

When the CNN job went away, I suddenly had the chance to ask myself what I really wanted to do.

A question I would've never asked, brought an answer I never expected.

I no longer wanted to do traditional news.

The idea of a job where I reported doom and gloom every day didn't seem like a match to where my head and heart were.

This is not to say my friends and family turned into a giant cheering section.

Frankly, they were shocked, worried and appalled.

"Er, do you not see how good you are at your job?" they pointed out. "Did you not notice the size of your news anchor paycheck? You could go get another job at Fox, MSNBC or a local news station."

True. True. And True. Except for one problem. I didn't want to do that anymore.

Rather, it was the inspiring stories were really making my heart go, "Zing!"

I created my website, DarynKagan.com, where every story fits the theme, "Show The World What's Possible!" I can now see the seeds of my new career chapter were in that "Your Spirit" segment I had created for my CNN show.

I also could've been sad about being single. The positive flip side was there was no husband to tell me I couldn't take this leap at my dream.

As for the kind of guy my war romance turned out to be, I cue up Garth Brooks, "Thank God For Unanswered Prayers."

The website and company have grown to include TV and radio projects, and now this newspaper column.

If you're in the midst of change that feels like it slapped your across the face like a flying frozen trout, might I suggest you go on your own archeological dig?

Are there signs that you've actually been getting ready?

Are there seeds of secret dreams you didn't even dare speak to yourself?

I keep a card on my desk that has helped me through many a difficult day. Written by the great Western author, Louis L'mour, it reads, "There will come a time when you believe everything is finished. That will be the beginning."

I've certainly felt that everything is finished.

The idea that the wrecking ball swinging at your life is the beginning of anything? That is a lot harder to sign up for.

Even harder—the idea that your new beginning was actually starting long before what right now feels like the end.

Take a second, fourth or forty sixth look.

It could be you've been getting ready all along.

Some stories can be explained.

Others just need to be told.

This is one such story.

It begins as I was getting ready to leave CNN and launch my own inspirational website. To produce stories and videos for DarynKagan.com I was going to need to learn how to shoot my own video. The cushy days of picking up the phone and requesting a three-person crew were about to end quickly.

Luckily, I knew just whom to ask to teach me how to shoot like a pro. Dan Young was my shooter when I traveled Africa covering the trip of U2's Bono and then US Treasury Secretary Paul O'Neill. Dan was always up for a challenge. No matter what someone would ask of him, his response always was, "Great! How can we get that done?!" He was always delighted and honored that you would ask him for help.

Shortly after our trip to Africa, Dan was promoted to CNN chief videographer. That made him the Grand Poobah, the Big Cheese in charge of every CNN videographer. The lofty status and management title didn't change Dan a bit. He was still the guy you always ask for help.

"I know," I thought in a flash of one of those light bulb moments. "I'll ask Dan for shooting lessons!"

A brilliant idea!

Sadly, it never happened.

Three weeks before I left CNN, Dan suddenly was diagnosed with leukemia. A week later he died. There are no words to describe how shocking it was. Vibrant, non-stop energy Dan dead at 47? It devastated the entire network. This wonderful, sunny man was gone way too soon.

His funeral was standing room only, even into the extra spillover room at the church. As I looked over at his wife, young son and twin brother, my heart ached for them, knowing my lost opportunity was nothing compared to their loss.

The next day in the CNN newsroom, I ran into another longtime CNN shooter, Dave Haeberlin. We hugged. We shared memories of Dan. Then, Dave asked me, "What's the project you're working on? Tell me about your website."

As I told him about DarynKagan.com a great idea suddenly popped into my head. I would now ask Dave for shooting lessons! Plan B! "Hey, Dave," I said. "I could actually use your help. I could use some shooting lessons."

That's when the inexplicable happened. Before I could finish explaining what I needed, Dave cut me off. "Dan took care of that," he said.

What? Clearly, Dave had misunderstood me.

"Dan took care of that," he repeated.

"How could that be?" I asked, thinking Dave must've misunderstood me. "I'd never had the chance to explain my website to Dan, let alone ask him for shooting lessons. How could have possibly taken care of it? "

Dave insisted that's exactly what Dan had done.

"I don't know how to explain it," Dave shook his head. "About two weeks ago, Dan sat down and wrote out a lesson plan detailing how to shoot a story so that it could be edited into a beautiful, professional-looking piece. I'll email it to you."

My jaw dropped as I looked at my computer screen. There it was—line for line the shooting lesson I needed. The way to frame a shot, the sequences, the necessary elements, how to hold a camera.

Through the words, through the excellent instruction, through my tears, I could feel Dan looking down on me with that delighted twinkle in his eye. "Great! We got it done!"

We sure did, my friend.

We sure did.

I Used To Be Someone

All I really wanted was a manicure.

Really, just about a half-hour to myself, a trim of some nasty hangnails and a couple coats of pretty light pink nail polish.

"Bubble Bath," I read on the bottom of the bottle, once I got out my reading glasses.

What I wasn't expecting was a punch in the gut.

"This is Daryn Kagan," the shop owner said the manicurist doing my nails. "She used to be someone."

There you have it.

It still makes me lean over and grab my middle to say it.

I remember thinking, "I know where she's going with this. I used to be a national news anchor on CNN."

In that respect, I guess, I did use to be someone.

Someone who I am not anymore.

I suspect I'm not alone.

I think there are a lot of us out there who used to be someone.

Someone's parent.

Someone's spouse.

Some big job that's no longer ours.

Losing my job a few years back—that was not my choice.

Not continuing to pursue a career where I got paid to talk about doom and gloom every single day—that was a conscious decision. And so, no, I am no longer someone.

Well, not the shop owner's idea of someone, anyway.

I think people like it when you fit into a single neat box. I rarely miss that, unless it's a moment when people want to label you easily.

"And now she is…?" the shop owner continued, eyebrows arched seeming to say, "help me here." She might as well have said "And now she is dot dot dot."

I can connect the dots when somebody cares enough or has the time to really want to know. I'm now somebody's wife and somebody's mother. I squeeze in time to be a columnist, run a website and do a TV show called, "Bookmark."

In other words, dot dot dot.

It's hard not to be someone anymore in the manicure shop.

It was hard at the new dentist's office the other day when I got to "Occupation" on the new patient form.

What do you write when you're not someone?

I knew the dentist didn't care about my dot dot dots. Certainly didn't leave enough space for anything more than a single word.

He just wanted to know if I had dental insurance.

I do not.

I did when I was someone. Does that count?

I will say this about all my dots—they fill my days and even more importantly, fill my heart.

A lot of people feel the need to replace their big label with running out and getting another one.

Gotta go be someone.

I suspect I won't be doing that, though there could be a few more dots in my future.

No, it's not easy to explain who I am these days. But I know I'm happier and my life is more interesting than when I was someone.

What about you?

Did you used to be someone?

I'd love to hear how you connect your dots.

That Time My Neighbors Dropped Off Some Unexpected Gifts

A couple of precious gifts from neighbors showed up at my front door this week.

No, not covered hot casseroles dishes so that I wouldn't have to cook dinner.

Though, that would've been nice.

All contributions are always graciously accepted.

This story starts with Eli.

You know all that stuff you hear about what's wrong with young people today?

None of it is true about Eli.

Here's a young man who put himself through college on scholarships.

The ink wasn't even dry on his diploma last summer when he already had an impressive first job.

"I'm helping to build apps at CNN," he told me when I ran into him a couple weeks ago.

"Why don't you stop by," I offered, "We'll talk about what your big dreams are and I'll see if I can help."

"What I really want to do is political news. I want to live in Washington, D.C.," he shared as we sat out on my front porch a few evenings later.

"How about I email some correspondents and executives I know in the CNN's DC bureau?" I offered.

Eli was momentarily speechless.

Was he trying to formulate a way to say, "Thank you?"

Turns out, at that moment, no.

Poor kid was in shock.

"You can do that? You can just email these people?" he said disbelieving.

That's when I realized.

To this 22-year-old young man, I'm just the crazy lady next door running around with my hair in a scrunchie.

Eli had dropped off at my front door the gift of remembering the fragments of a life chapter gone by.

For me, my 12-years as a news anchor at CNN.

Before marriage and kids became my lead story.

Perhaps, a similar thing has happened to you, Dear Reader.

A reminder that you are no longer someone who you used to be.

Not someone's wife.

Not someone's mom or dad.

Not that person on your old business card, back in the days when people carried business cards.

Even when you think you don't miss the old life, the reminder of you're not any longer can sting, especially when you used to be something or someone you and others considered kind of special.

I was sharing the story with my neighbor, Sam, who has known me through each phase of the last 16 years.

"You should've seen the look on Eli's face," I laughed. "He thinks I'm just the crazy lady next door. He doesn't know I used to have a life."

"No, you used to have a fancy career," Sam corrected me. "Now, you have a life."

Ah, for the gifts of perspective from sweet neighbors.

All is good on the block.

Well, except for one thing.

Eli's dream job?

The one in DC.

Turns out he got it.

My email introductions might have had helped. Truthfully, he's the kind of person who is going places with or without an assist from me.

In fact, he's already gone.

His mother hasn't stopped weeping.

I'm now the lady who helped send her kid away.

I don't think she'll be dropping dinner off anytime soon.

Breaking Up With The Checklist

It was one of the biggest break ups of my life.

If I'm honest with you, Dear Reader, I must tell you there are times when I'm still not over this great love.

There are days, well, no, okay, at least moments, where I look over my shoulder and wonder, "Maybe we could try one more time to make this work?"

This time, I have Robin Williams to thank for setting me straight.

For the love, the pull, the temptation are all tied to, not a person.

No something much greater than just one person.

For years I was in love with Checklist.

We were together for years, Checklist and I.

Checklist offered up guidance and hope.

Once, and only once, I'd checked off certain life events and accomplishments would I be happy.

And so I chased.

Chased love.

Chased success.

Chased money.

Chased having a family.

Chased having the perfect house.

Maybe you've had a similar relationship, Dear Reader? Your own list you've chased with singular focus?

"Keep going!" My List encouraged me over the years. "You can do it! Only then will you reach happy!"

Turns out, Checklist is a cruel life partner.

The more I chased, the more he added on, like teaching a kid to swim, telling them they just have a few strokes to your safe and loving arms, but you keep stepping back, back, back.

And of course, while I chased, I looked and compared myself to others.

Others, who had checked and accomplished so much more.

"Gotta do all this to be happy!"

"Gotta catch up with the others!" I told myself.

Somewhere, in this chase, the cracks started to move through this great love affair.

"Maybe instead of chasing happy," it occurred to me, "I could simply choose to be happy now with what I have."

And so, we broke up Checklist and I.

Funny thing happened with that radical move—some of those long elusive longings—love, family, children?

They got checked.

I'm not perfect.

I have those days, ok, moments when I think, "Maybe I'll be happier when I accomplish this or that."

Who doesn't do that?

Who doesn't look at the next guy who has checked so much more?

Which brings me to Robin Williams.

His recent death brought powerful lessons.

After all, who better to envy than Robin Willams?

King of The Checklist!

Talent-check.

Money-check.

Family-three wives, three kids. That's a lot of love.

Success-check check check check.

And yet, I read stories his real life, of his heart, of his struggles.

Robin Williams sounded absolutely miserable.

I will think of him every time I look over my shoulder, or at the next person, or at something or someone that I think I need to be happy.

Thank you, Robin Williams, for reminding me that chasing my checklist, envying what someone else has is an empty game.

I don't know what anyone has.

And Checklist-though you taunt me, try to lure me back, the best thing I ever checked off—breaking up with you.

When No One Else Hears Your Rattle

Have you heard my rattle?

The one that's driving me crazy?

It's happening in my new car.

Well, not that new.

The car's about a year and a half old.

Old enough to start with quirks.

Too new, if you ask me, to already have a rattle.

When I take the car out on the highway and get it up to speed, it sounds like the right front passenger window starts to rattle.

Only it doesn't.

See, it's not the window, we've checked that, but it comes from that general area.

The *knocka-thumpa-knocka-thumpa* sound really bugs me.

Even worse, it drives my noise-sensitive husband through the sunroof.

So off I went this week to the dealership.

I waited and waited like the hostage you become in a dealership waiting room.

A guy finally comes in, apologetic, yet with that "Grey's Anatomy" we've done all we can do" looks on his face.

"I can't hear your rattle," he says.

"Let's take a drive," I suggest, ready to rattle his world.

We drive up and down the highway at all sorts of speeds.

I'll be darned if I suddenly can't hear the rattle either.

It was as if the Maytag Man came to life in my car.

Just like the classic TV commercial, the car rattled until he shows up.

Talk about frustrating.

"Oh well," the dealership guy says as he gives me that, "It's time for you to go home now, Crazy Lady" look.

"What's the big deal?" I ask myself as I drive off. "How lucky are you that this is your biggest problem today?"

Only, suddenly, I picture the two-hour road trip we will be taking this weekend to see my in-laws, the rattle starting in, Husband going on edge and I know this will be a bigger problem within a few days.

As I continue to stress about the mystery rattle, it strikes me, Dear Reader, you just might have a rattle, as well.

Maybe not in your kinda, newish car. Rather, that thing that is the thorn in your side, that others can't see or detect that you're told to get over.

The heartbreak that others believe you should be passed already.

The chronic pain that doesn't go away from a long ago injury.

The brain injury that doesn't show on the outside, but completely rewired you and your life forever.

The cancer you survived, but leaves you feeling unsettled.

Your rattle.

Like the guy at the car dealership, I can't fix your rattle.

But I offer you today, this tiny gift—

I'm validating your rattle.

I hear it.

I see it.

I feel it.

I believe it's there.

I hope this moment of understanding and acknowledgement gives you some comfort.

For just a moment, you're not that crazy person.

Speaking of comfort—

I hate to ask--

Any chance you have a car I can borrow Saturday to go see my in-laws?

One without a rattle, of course.

For the sake of my sanity and my marriage, I would be ever so appreciative.

The Stumble That Humbled Me

I fell this week.

By that, I mean, I fell.

Literally, fell.

Flat.

It happened as I was just starting a little run, jog, or "shuffle" as my kids call it.

That's when I spotted a neighbor watering his lawn.

I turned to say hello, focusing on the pretty flowers instead of the sidewalk in front of me.

That's all it took.

My big ol' right foot caught a crack in the sidewalk and I launched.

Felt like it took about 10 minutes for me to fly through the air, landing splat on the ground.

The US Olympic Diving Team is not on the phone trying to recruit me for my gracefulness, as I had not one bit.

Four days later, I'm walking around with a swollen knee devoid of skin covering, scraped elbows, hand, belly and upper thigh. And as I do, as I clean up my wounds, wonder about that swelling under my kneecap, it occurs to me.

I'm probably not the only one who fell this week.

It's possible, Dear Reader, you did, too.

Chances are you stayed physically up right on your two appropriately, sized feet. But in this tricky, perilous, entangled world of ours, there are so many ways to fall.

Maybe for you it was falling off that new diet plan you swore was going to be the one. Maybe you surfed that old love on social media. Maybe your kid told you how much they hate you and you can't really blame them because you're not a perfect parent. Maybe, you got laid off from that job you loved. Maybe, it was Tuesday that you couldn't get out of bed because your grief is just too big. Yeah, that grief that your friends and family figure you should be past by now.

Yeah, you fell.

The answer is, "three."

Just in case you were wondering how many neighbors saw me go splat on my face.

Which is the other part of falling.

The witnesses.

Those neighbors saw me fall also saw me do the only thing I knew to at the time.

I heard my late father's voice in my head. "Get up and walk it off," he always said.

And so, I did.

The getting up was about as graceful as the fall.

One awkward wobble, in shock, trying to regain my breath which remained knocked out on the sidewalk.

But I got up, darn it. I did.

I share for two simple reasons.

First, you might want to buy stock in bandages and hydrogen peroxide because to see my mess of a body, is to know sales will be booming.

And mainly, I share for you.

You, who also fell, in one way or another, this week.

My wish for you is that you were able to get up and walk it off.

And if you weren't quite able to yet.

I hope that walk comes soon.

It doesn't have to be pretty.

Life is a trip.

We all fall down.

The Best Wrinkle I Ever Found

"I see wrinkles on your forehead!"

The words were coming from my beau, Mr. SummerFest.

Honestly they were almost too beautiful to believe.

They came amidst the past couple of weeks where my concept of what is beautiful has been turned upside down.

My lesson in what's really beautiful began a couple Fridays ago as I felt a recurring twitching in my upper right lip. It happened to be the day we were shooting our weekly videos for my website DarynKagan.com, so I asked my photographer, Brian, "Does my face look funny?"

He got that look on his face that men do when you ask them things like, "Do these jeans make my butt look big?"

It's that look that shows no matter what they say, this won't end well.

"Nope. Your face looks great in person and on camera," was his safe reply.

"Sweet," I thought. "And a big ol' lie."

Something wasn't right.

By Sunday night the right side of my face was gone.

Well, not gone, per say. It was there next to the left side of my face, but there was nothing I could do with it. I couldn't move a muscle, not even to blink my right eye.

I did what most of us medically uneducated people do when it appears something is going terribly wrong—I headed to the internet for self-diagnosis.

I imagine most people look for the worst.

Personally, I don't have time or desire for the worst, so I skipped brain tumors and strokes and headed straight for "Bell's Palsy."

I had remembered my friend, Dan, describing similar symptoms when this happened to him a few years ago. Sure enough, there on the Web MD website were all my symptoms: weakness or paralysis of one side of the face, tearing eye, frozen eyelid. Check, check, check.

The website explained that this could be caused by a virus to the nerves that control the facial muscles, or not. It could take a week or six months to get better.

I chose a week.

I am so thankful that it is not something more serious. Still, it's apparent, Mr. Bell and his palsy showed up to teach me quite a few lessons, the first being patience. Some things will get better on their own time. I'm well into Week Two and while I've had great improvement with the help of good medical care, I'm still not all the way back.

Most of all, it has been a lesson in appreciation. The things we take for granted—something so simple as being able to blink and close my eye. That would be more valuable to me than the finest jewels in the world.

And wrinkles? I know plenty of you ladies out there pay the big bucks to make your wrinkles go away. Right now, I can't imagine anything more beautiful to see some on the right side of my face. It means the muscle function is coming back. It means I'm getting better.

That's why each day I pull my hair back and with all my might and concentration try to wrinkle my forehead like the doctor asked me to when she confirmed the Bell's Palsy diagnosis. That day in the emergency room, my left side was properly crinkled, while my right stayed as flat and smooth as a glass bottom boat.

"Do you see any wrinkles?" I ask Mr. SummerFest with great hope each day.

"I think I do!" he says though I'm not sure if he's being honest or just encouraging.

Maybe you're having one of those days where you can't stand what you see in the mirror. What do you do with a face you think looks older or a new sagging area you hadn't noticed before?

It's simple.

Do something for me.

Go back to that mirror, blink both your eyes and give thanks for the beauty that is your face.

From where I sit with one eye wide open, that one blink is more incredible than any cream, injection or surgery could ever create.

A definite wrinkle in what I used to consider beautiful.

Dancing Alone

My husband is still laughing at this.

Well, laughing at me.

Story goes back to a few years ago when we were dating, snuggled up on the couch watching "Dancing With The Stars." Husband sweetly asked me, "Would you ever want to take ballroom dance lessons?"

I thought about it a second and responded, "You mean, together?"

He still howls at this because, as he points out, how else do you take ballroom dance lessons? Who takes ballroom dance lessons alone?

Uh, that would be me.

When you're single as long as I was, when you constantly picked guys who didn't do more than toss a few cookie crumbs of their time your way, you learn to do a lot of stuff by yourself.

Yes, including sign up for ballroom dance lessons.

I got thinking about this the other day when I came across this study which confirms Husband's theory that he married a different bird. A business professor at the University of Maryland says Americans are not going out, if that means having to go out alone.

Does this sound like you, Dear Reader?

Where do you draw your line in the comfort zone sand?

Would you go out to a restaurant by yourself?

To a movie?

Take dance lessons?

According to this study, most of you won't if it means going solo.

The reason?

You're too worried about what other people would think.

Here's the punch line on that one—

Another study shows people aren't watching you. They're not judging you, probably because they're too busy being self-conscious about what people are thinking about them!

Seems to me, we all have some kind of challenge to overcome to live our lives more fully.

For me, it has been getting used to a whole cookie kind of guy. A man who wants to spend a lot of time with me and go do stuff.

Yes, together.

They really do make guys like that. Who knew? Certainly not me until well into my 40's.

And you?

You need to get over yourself and those imaginary people who, I promise, will not be judging you if you get out there by yourself for dinner, a movie, or even dance lessons.

And then there's this—

When that hottie instructor is twirling you across the ballroom floor as the music makes a symphony in your heart, the last thing you will be thinking about is being alone.

I know because I've certainly danced that dance.

The last laugh is going to be all yours.

The Gift Of Crummy Holidays

I've figured out the perfect gift!

It's perfect for--

Well, everybody.

That's why I am now committing to a crummy holiday season.

Okay, maybe not the whole season,

But at least a couple of days.

A few failure moments.

You know me, Dear Reader.

I'm all about gratitude, being happy with what you have.

But a line is gets crossed this time of year.

To go on Facebook, to open your mailbox is to be deluged with perfection!

Everyone's children are straight-A darlings who never so much as roll a single eyeball.

Everyone's home is decorated with 22 Christmas trees and the 44 holiday cookies they made are from scratch. No Pillsbury Dough Boy shortcuts for them!

Everyone's spouse is their best friend who picked out the perfect gift.

In a word, "Puh-lease."

It's enough to make a relatively happy person gag and wonder, "Why aren't my holidays all that?"

And then, there are the folks I'm really hurting for.

I have family and friends, acquaintances, who are having a hard time this year.

First year without a loved one.

Tough financial times.

I have one friend who is still watching the ink dry on her divorce papers.

"Facebook," she gulped to me the other day as we dunked our feet in pedicure tubs trying to wash our troubles away. "I, pictures, happy, everyone, cry…"

She couldn't put the words together in a sentence, but I knew what she meant.

Sharing your fake perfect happiness is making someone else miserable.

Can we just for one day be honest?

After all, even if things are pretty good for this year, you know you've been in a place where they have not.

So how about the gift everyone can love?

The gift of imperfection.

My friend, Jen, was a great Imperfection Gift Giver describing her Thanksgiving on Facebook.

"Fights over who would make the place cards for the table, tears over forts destroyed by mischievous little brothers and a little over-the-top 'tween dramatics to keep it interesting. No doubt, that's exactly how the first Thanksgiving was spent."

You know I clicked a "Like" button on that one!

I can add that I managed to overcook the pre-cooked turkey I bought for our Thanksgiving.

That takes astounding talent, yes, I know.

I pause a moment while I take a bow.

If you need it I can provide a list of at least 18 family and friends who we are disappointing by not seeing them this holiday season.

Decorations? I only put away the Thanksgiving decorations (two stuffed animal turkeys) last week.

Bad Mommy might really not get around to getting that fresh tree up or lighting the Menorah eight nights. Talk about an equal opportunity screw up.

If this is truly your crummiest holiday season ever, the good news is future holidays can be a lot better.

And when they are, it'll be your turn to share that hope, that things can get better, just make sure you keep it real.

Better isn't perfect.

But imperfection will always be the perfect gift.

Get Him Out Of My Bed

I'm struggling with a relationship I never wanted to get into.

It's a betrayal to everything good that I cherish in my life.

It's not where I want to spend a moment of my time.

Yet, he comes each night.

Or make that morning, as he usually shows up around 3 am.

Sometimes, it's 3:12.

Sometimes, he waits until 3:28.

Last night, he was particularly excited to get things going and woke me up at 2:58.

I call him, "The Night Devil."

He's the one who pulverizes my daytime candy-coated illusion of having things all together.

Night Devil can rouse me from a peaceful sleep with a bad dream or a sudden thought that I'm falling off a cliff.

And once I'm awake, I'm all his as he loves to toss my anxieties around the room like a frenzied toddler whipping toys out of giant toy box.

"What's this?" He holds up an image of my upcoming trip. "Let's stress about all that go wrong!"

"Wait, let's get freaked out about the kids! Are they happy? How are their grades? Will they be safe while I'm gone?"

"Wee! This is fun! How about that deadline for the edits on your first novel? What made you think you could ever do this in the first place?"

"Ooh, look over here—How's your Mom doing? What if something happens to her while you're out of the country?"

Night Devil delights in my endless list of worries.

Worries which somehow seem manageable by day. The bright light he shines on them makes them seem a lot scarier in the middle of the night.

I have to believe Night Devil and I are not in an exclusive relationship.

Is it just me or do you have a similar nightly visitor, Dear Reader?

What time does he show up in your bedroom?

I know from tossing and turning that my husband's visitor shows up around 4 am.

I turn over and see him scanning websites on his phone.

"This is what relaxes me," he insists, knowing I think that's a silly way to get back to sleep.

Only one thing works for me, a game taught to me by my friend, Tricia.

"The Gratitude Alphabet Game," she calls it. "Go through each letter of the alphabet naming something you're grateful for."

"Antiques Road Show, barre exercise classes, chocolate chip cookies..."

Hey, I didn't claim to be exciting or sophisticated, just freaked out in the middle of the night.

Indeed, Night Devil hates the Gratitude game, finds it quite boring, and leaves me long before I get to Z.

Which of course, is ultimately what I am thankful for—returning to "zzzzzz's."

Whatever sleep I'm able to seize back before I need to get up at 5:14 will help me up for another day.

D is for the day so gratefully busy that I can keep my anxieties stuffed down where I prefer them.

I can ignore my unwanted visitor until he shows up again tonight. Unless, that is, you know of a way I can make him accept he's not welcome in my bedroom ever again.

One Stupid Thing To Stop Saying

Of all the cliché news phrases that drive me nuts, and trust me, there are more than a few—

You can put up at the top of the list, "He lost his battle with cancer."

Please.

We need to stop.

Just stop saying this.

Dear Reader, if your email to me is any indication, you get it.

Ever since I began to share my mom's journey of her recent diagnosis with lymphoma you have avalanched me with your story.

With your mom's story.

With your child's story.

With your sister's story.

There are no shortage of cancer stories out there.

And so many brave warriors.

The lengths the ones you love go to fight cancer is amazing, inspiring, hopeful and daunting.

There is not a single loser among you.

I found a powerful, slap me across the face reminder the other day.

Surely, you've heard about the recent passing of ESPN sportscaster, Stuart Scott.

He was a broadcasting trailblazer I met few times in my career, though I would be over-embellishing to call him more than the good friend of some friends of mine.

Still, he caught my attention last year with his remarkable acceptance speech as he received the "Jimmy V Award for Perseverance," honoring him for the way he was battling through three rounds of cancer.

He's the one who convinced me to lose the idea of losing.

Stuart said, "When you die, it does not mean that you lose to cancer. You beat cancer by how you live, why you live, and in the manner in which you live."

Boy, did he live.

Boy, are so many of you.

Living in the way you stare cancer in the face.

Living in the way you take on surgery, chemo and radiation.

Living in the way you now appreciate each day and moment in a way you never did before.

Living in the way you leave nothing left unsaid to those that you love.

I know because you've taken the time to drop me a line and share your challenges, your fears, your triumphs.

I know because you've taken the time to share with me the lives and stories of someone you've loved who has passed.

You school me each day that yep, cancer sure does suck. It is something you would never pick. It rearranges what you had planned for your life.

And then you show me that through all that, you choose to be the kind of person you want to be.

That is where the true power lies.

In the person who fights.

In the loved one who turns into a Super Hero caretaker.

I am humbled, educated and inspired.

The idea that you might lose, that anyone lost a battle to cancer—

Please, please, just stop.

For all who have fought and are fighting.

For all who are taking care of your loved one, I hereby declare the score:

You: 1,000

Cancer: Big Fat Zero.

My Dog. Always
My Dog

"DarlaDog on her afternoon walk, telling me, in her way that she's happy
to sit on the grass and let the wafting breezes bring the smells to her."

I learned something new about one of my favorite people in the world this
week.

By favorite people, I mean my dog.

You don't see dogs as people and think those us who do are on the wrong
side of crazy? Save your time, read no more.

But if you're like me and know your dog is a member of your family, your
baby, your soul sister, then, yes, read on.

I heard about this contraption where you soon will be able to speak English
with your dog. The device fits on your dog's head like a telemarketer's headset.
Researchers in Europe believe they can make it analyze your dog's brain waves
and translate those thoughts in language we humans can understand.

What a silly premise behind this invention! Ten bucks says the inventor doesn't have a dog of his own.

It is indeed true my dog, Darla, has never spoken a human word.

But what have we been doing these last 14 years since I brought her home from the Humane Society, if not having one long, amazing awesome, life-affirming conversation?

There are the basics that need to be covered like DarlaDog communicating,

"Scratch my ear, please."

"What's for dinner?"

"There are some awesome smells on our street just waiting for us to take a walk."

"You really don't want to date that guy." (Should've listened more closely to that one a few times.)

"The new 3-legged cat is kind of cool. We should keep her." (Perhaps we should've spoken more on that last one. Turns out, the cat is nuts.)

And then, of course, the best, conversations of all, when I snuggle down close to Darla's snout and she peers at me with those dark brown eyes. If there are words that express the unconditional, intensely devoted love my dog speaks to me, I have not learned them yet.

There is no question in my heart, the conversation has been had.

I imagine you've had equally wonderful conversations with your dog, as well.

I told my husband about this new device and asked him, "What do you think Darla would say if she could talk?"

"That's easy," he replied in his straightforward manner, "Food, food, food. Oh, and Mama."

He knows us well, that husband of mine, even if he has to learn to speak Dog.

"I tried to take Darla for a walk," he complained the other day. "She won't go."

"She wants you to scratch her belly first," I said from the other room without looking up from book I was reading.

"How do you know that?" he asked.

"Dunno. She told me once, I guess."

Sure enough, he walked back, Darla rolled over four legs and belly in the air.

"Now that we're clear on that, let's go for a walk," she groaned as pushed back on her not so strong, old lady back legs.

"Come here, I'll put your leash on," Husband said, expecting Darla to come his way.

"She doesn't understand what you're saying," I yelled from the other room.

"How do you know?"

"Well, for one, she's almost 14 and she's deaf," I explained. "And the way you talk to her just sounds like the 'Waah Waah' sound like the teacher in Charlie Brown cartoons."

"What?" he said totally confused.

Makes perfect sense to me. A year into marriage, I'm still working on learning to speak Husband language fluently. But Dog? Got that one down.

Think I'll save my money.

I won't be buying that Dog Translation contraption when it comes out.

Go spend it on dog treats instead.

Darla tells me she thinks that's a fine idea.

Old Dog Love

Many days she smells no better than an old blanket that's been soaking in a bucket of sour milk for week.

Her body sports more lumps than a bride's first attempt at making mashed potatoes.

Still, I look at her and know that I'm in love.

She is my 14 ½ year old dog.

Together, we've reached a bittersweet chapter.

I now know Old Dog Love.

Our story goes back to the year 2000. I was single and living alone when my house was broken into. Three days later, the thugs came back and stole my car off the street using a set of spare car keys I hadn't realized they had taken.

The police shrugged their shoulders. "Lady, get a gun or get a dog," was their big advice.

Since I'd never even held a gun, my choice was clear.

I headed to the Humane Society where I knew her the moment I saw her—a delicious ball of yellow fur rolling around showing off her pink belly. "Lab Mix," the sign in front of the litter said.

"How very generous," I've thought about that description over the years, realizing my dog is much more "mix" than "Lab."

Turns out, needing some protection was just the excuse to lead me to one of the best relationships of my life.

We had Puppy Love, which is much like it sounds. A crush on someone who loves you instantly, unconditionally, and ultimately unrealistically.

That led to Teen Dog Love where I realized my dog wasn't perfect, needed guidance to stay out of trouble, but so fun because she was always up for adventure be it countless hours in the dog park, a swim in a river, or a trip to the beach.

And there's been plenty of Full Grown Love, when it seems she has just always been here. She's known me as the single career girl, met and sniffed out various beaus.

When I married last year, she effortlessly made the transition to Family Dog, somehow charming my previously non-animal loving husband. If we both are in the house, but in separate rooms, she makes a point to go lay by his feet, instead of mine.

When I go check on them, she gives me that dog wink as if to say, "I got this." My otherwise astute husband has no clue he's been suckered into a special friendship.

My dog is 14 ½ now and I know our time together is shorter rather than longer.

It's in the way I give her back legs a boost to hop into the back seat of the car.

It's in the way our three long daily walks have been replaced by one. She much prefers her day-long snoring snooze fest in her self-created cave behind the couch in the den.

It's in the neighborhood news that other dogs she played with in the park as a puppy have passed on.

I know in my head, the contract she signed to be on this Earth is shorter than mine. Yet, the idea of her passing on instantly fills my eyes with buckets of tears and makes it a little hard to breathe.

If you're a person whose heart is being kept by a dog, I know you understand.

That's why every chance I get, I drink in that stinky smell like it's the world's finest perfume and run my hands over her lumpy body.

It's a case of Old Dog Love.

And I got it bad.

We Have A Teen Sass Problem In Our Family

We have a sass problem in our family.

Teenaged sass.

Talk back, argue, and try to negotiate every boundary kind of sass.

"Take away their iPads!" you suggest.

"Send them to their rooms!" you insist.

Thank you very much for your parenting input.

Thing is…

The sass, well, it's not coming from either of the two teenagers who make their home under our roof.

It's coming from—

The cat.

The 3-legged cat.

Pisa is her name. As in "Leaning Tower of---"

The cat, who if I'm honest, I will admit, is result of a rebound relationship.

Tripod was my first three-legged cat.

My great love for 19 years!

You, fellow animal lover, can imagine the hole in my heart when 'Pod died.

Four months after 'Pod passed, I got an email.

It came from a local cat rescue group and went something like, "We heard you are the crazy cat lady who takes in 3-legged cats. We have this cat we've tried to place for more than two years, perhaps you could see it in your crazy cat lady heart to take her in."

"I'm not ready for another cat," I warned but I can come meet her."

I know. I know. You're laughing already.

Truth is, this was not love at first sight.

"I guess I could 'foster' her for a bit," I said hesitantly as they shoved me out the door, cat carrier in hand.

"She sure talks a lot," I confessed to my even more animal loving sister.

"That's just her settling in," she assured me. "She'll be better in six months."

Wrong.

Five years later, I can tell you this is like having the late Joan Rivers in a cat, "Can we talk?"

"Can we talk about food at 5:30?"

5:30, as in a.m.

"Can we talk about how I want to be held?"

"Can we talk about how I want to go outside?"

To not engage or even worse, not meet Pisa's request, is to hear the sass, the negotiating, or if she's feeling extra emotional, to be treated to a recounting of her two plus years in the cat shelter.

Imagine a 10-minute out-of-tune meow in C-sharp.

The question becomes, Dear Reader, what to do with a sassy cat who has a lot to say?

My husband has some ideas, few of which are legal or involve keeping the cat.

The kids have learned how to cradle Pisa like a newborn baby, which does quiet the cat, but tends to put a crimp in things like homework, their social lives, and taking a bath.

The dog is happiest because at 14 1/2, she's deaf.

Lucky dog.

And so I put it to you?

Dear Reader, do you have a conversationalist cat?

Husband thinks I'm part of the problem.

That I've spoiled the cat.

Can you imagine?!

Any ideas?

Set Pisa and me straight at Daryn@DarynKagan.com.

Just make sure you speak up, so that I can hear you over all the meowing.

The Tommy Dozen

Leave it to a bunch of chickens to teach me a lesson.

About gratitude.

About what is enough.

About what makes a party.

Yes, I did say, "chickens."

As in the 7 crazy chickens I have living in our backyard.

Got my first chickens about four years ago, the day before my first date with my now husband. That was one lucky week.

Let's get right to it.

Folks always want to know do we get fresh eggs?

Sure do.

The chicken math adds up to about an egg every other day from each lady.

Sometimes more. Sometimes less, depending on their mood, luck, time of the year, the stock market.

And nothing, by that, I mean nothing, makes a better "Thank you," gift than a dozen fresh eggs.

Invite me to your house for dinner? I'll show up with a dozen fresh eggs. You'll go nuts.

Which leads me to last year, when my father-in-law wanted to come to see our daughter in her school orchestra recital. He and his wife live a couple hours away. He wasn't up for doing the driving. His wife wasn't feeling tip top either.

"No problem," says Tommy. Tommy, who happens to be a friend from church. Tommy says, "I'll drive you up."

Two hours each way to sit and listen to someone else's grandkid's squeaky orchestral recital? Yes, we're talking true friend.

No better way to say, "Thank you," I figured, than send Tommy home with a dozen fresh eggs.

One problem.

I looked at my stash in the fridge to find I only had 11.

What could I do? How rude to give only 11 eggs!

"C'mon, Ladies," I implored as I popped out to the chicken coop. "Surely, you can lay one more egg? One more egg for Mr. Tommy?"

The chickens paid me no mind. Ignored me, as they do when there is something delicious that deserves their attention more.

There was a heaping pile of what you and I would call trash.

Put it down your garbage disposal.

If you're green, perhaps, in a compost heap.

When you have chickens, you toss it the chickens' way—stale bread, over-soft tomatoes, apple peels and such.

And therein lies the lesson:

What is trash to me, is treasure to the chickens.

A party! A fiesta! A moment to be excited about what has come their way.

That's when it clicked.

I went back inside, packed up the 11 eggs in a carton.

"We have a new tradition!" I declared as I met up with Pops and Tommy. "Many have received a dozen eggs," I explained to our guest. "You are the first, however, to receive a 'Tommy Dozen!'"

I opened the carton to show only 11 eggs.

Tommy's reaction?

What do you expect from a man who would drive a buddy to his grand-daughter's recital in another state?

Tommy, being Tommy, howled with laughter.

He was delighted and honored.

Took those 11 eggs and headed back down to their hometown.

I hear The Tommy Dozen story has now been told many times at their church.

It's become part of our family lingo.

You might not have all that you expected or counted on, but look at it the right way and you'll see you have enough.

A bounty.
A party.
A fiesta.
For that, I thank the chickens.
And Tommy.

My Dog Leads The Way To Joy

To chore or not to chore.

That is the question.

The debate between people like me.

Crazy mad dog lover.

And people like my husband.

People who don't get the whole dog thing.

Such people exist.

Who knew?

Certainly not me, until I married one.

"Have you done your chores this morning?" he'll ask.

Let me translate:

"Have I walked you walked the dog?"

No matter how I try to explain, he just doesn't get the concept.

Walking my dog is not a chore.

It is, simply, Joy.

I love watching the way her tail wags to a certain beat.

The flap, flap, flapping of the fold of her ears as she bounces down the street.

Even the way she overcomes the slight limp from the arthritis in her left hip.

The way she turns back about every 12 feet just to check on me to make sure I'm still there.

There's the fun of running into other dog friends.

You know the kind—you remember the name of the dog, but for the life of you, you can't remember the name of their human.

Complete awkwardness, of course, is running into the same human without their dog, like in the grocery store. "Oh hello, uh, Pepper's mom!" is the best improvisation I can come up with.

But back to our dog walk, Dear Fellow Dog Lover Reader.

I tried taking Husband on these walks. Surely, he would see the joy.

Nope.

He was fidgety.

The walk was something to be endured like getting through a traffic jam, just wanting to get home.

Darla and I now leave him home.

I'm betting you understand.

It's possible you get the same daily joy with your dog?

The time you would never set aside to get that breath of fresh air.

To let your wind wander.

To just be.

It's when I'm able to dream up ideas.

Stuck for a topic for this column?

I simply leash up Darla and head out for a smile and inspiration.

Oh, sweet Darla Dog.

She's going 15 years old now.

Our walks are so much shorter than they were when she was a pup.

Used to be, we'd have to walk an hour through three different neighborhood parks just to get out all her puppy energy.

These days, she often snores her way through our afternoon walk, figuring the front steps won't be worth the effort.

"One less chore," my husband would say.

"Hardly," I say.

More like a day with 15 minutes fewer joy.

Think I'll grab Darla's leash and we'll head out to think about this a little more.

My Dog Is Teaching Me A Final Lesson

My dog is getting me ready.

She knows what's coming in the way dogs know before we do.

About a dangerous stranger, earthquakes, or bacon.

She's gently letting me know it will soon be time for her to go.

It's one of an infinite number of brilliant conversations I've had with my best friend.

The friend who has never uttered a word in our more than 15 years together, but has taught me so much.

"She's not going anywhere," Husband tries to soothe and reassure me.

I appreciate this man who is wise in so many things. I also know he doesn't speak Dog.

She's letting me know in the way she's eased me back from three, to two, to one walk a day, like weaning a toddler from multiple naps.

The way her back legs get a little weaker every day.

The way she's had a few accidents.

Hers is not a straight decline.

She's had some senior moments followed by some almost puppy like days, well, moments actually, if I'm being honest.

More than anything, it's the look in her eyes. The look that says, "You've done so much for me these last 15 years, but you're going to have to do one more. I didn't sign up to be here as long as you did. You're going to have to let me go."

I know she's not the dog who will want heroic measures.

The folks down the street are paying huge vet bills to give their dog chemo. I get it.

I've had that pet.

My first 3-legged cat was that way. A trip to the vet was an excuse to go for a ride in the car and get cuddles from the vet techs. He was up for every treatment to keep him here 20 years.

Not this dog. She has hated the vet since her first puppy shots. Any trip there has always been agony.

Even my wonderful vet reminded me of this when I called him a couple weeks ago when Darla was having a bad day.

"I'm happy to look at her," he said. "But if you're clear she won't want anything done, why are you bringing her in?"

Thank God for a vet who turns away a chance to make a buck, who helps save Darla from my selfish wish to keep her here forever.

I know there's a chance, you understand, Dear Reader.

That you've had to say, "Goodbye" to your best friend, too.

If you've done it before, like I did with Tripod, you can see signs you denied the last time.

Now, I can listen.

The master teacher is giving one last lesson.

Make her comfortable.

Enjoy every single walk, snuggle, and slurpy kiss.

It could be our last.

I look deep into her cloudy chocolate brown eyes, pools of love and wisdom, for the strength to give her the gift she's earned a million times over the last 15 years.

The strength to let her go when it's her time.

So, About My Best Friend

My husband thinks he caught me.

Cheating on him, actually.

I can assure you, there was no cheat.

Nothing behind his back.

Everything was and is out in the open.

In front of you, actually.

Perhaps you caught my column about a month ago about dog's final chapter.

Most readers, probably, you the fellow dog lover, got swept up in the emotion of the idea that you, too, will one day have to say, "Goodbye," to your best friend.

And there you have it.

The catch.

Those two words.

Perhaps you understand, Dear Reader.

What it is to have a special person in your life who doesn't understand your enthusiastic, perhaps they'd say, "wacko" love for your pets.

Being married to an avowed non-animal lover means having to explain a language of love they don't understand.

"I saw your column," he said the day it came out.

Did he weep too about the idea of losing 15-year-old DarlaDog.

No, he's convinced she will out live all of us.

"I saw you wrote about your 'best friend.'"

I looked at him blankly. What was his point?

"Your 'best friend?'" he repeated.

"Oh, you're hurt that I didn't call you my best friend?" I asked, thinking that couldn't possibly be where he was going with this.

"Well, that is the idea, isn't it? Your husband is your best friend?"

It's a conversation I've tried to explain with him since I've known him.

I believe animal lovers simply have a different chamber of our heart that can only be filled up with the love we have and get from our pets.

I certainly am not he first to call my dog my best friend.

Lest you think Husband is some unfeeling jealous fool, let me assure you, he is the one who is getting caught.

Caught taking the animals under his wing, so to speak.

"I'm sad," he texted me one morning while I was out of town on for work. "The big chickens are being bullies and not letting little Nugget eat all her breakfast."

Or the ongoing debate on whether Darla should be allowed behind the couch in the den.

"She has limited days left. She should be allowed to live them out where she wants," he demanded sounding more like the animal crazy than me.

The way he's grown, the way he's taken on my animals has only made me love me more in the three years we've been married.

You could even say he has grown into my best friend.

My best human friend.

Don't tell him though.

Wouldn't want to get caught.

My Dog's Getting The Last Laugh

Let me say, Dear Reader, that you are amazing.

Wonderful.

Clearly, you're an over the top dog lover, like myself.

The emails have been flooding in ever since I shared the latest chapter of my sweet Darla's life in the column, "My Dog Is Teaching Me A Final Lesson."

I shared how my dog has been showing signs of slowing down, how she's preparing me to let her go after more than 15 years together.

I know, you can't even think about that with your own dog without pulling out a tissue or a bucket or swimming pool to catch your tears.

You've been so sweet to share with me the story of your dog. Of the great love you shared. Of his or her final days. Of how hard it is to say, "Goodbye," to your best friend.

You've also been wonderful in offering advice. Ways to have the vet come over, books to read, videos to watch, poems to read. The time you've taken to help me cope and ultimately grieve has been humbling and overwhelming.

Which leads me to the thing I feel compelled to share this week.

Something I need to let you know, because, well, you and I have that kind of relationship.

See the thing is, my dog is alive.

Not just alive.

Very much alive.

Yes, she's still over 15 years old. Still deaf. And was definitely having some struggles.

But it seems since I wrote that column a couple weeks ago, Darla has undergone a renaissance of sorts. It's kind of like when you call the dishwasher repairman and have him show up only to watch the darn machine work just fine.

I wake up to emails, texts and phone calls bemoaning Darla's passing, only to see a dog scrambling to get to the front door for our daily walk.

It's as if she's living the old quote, "Reports of my death have been greatly exaggerated."

Darla gets the last laugh.

And why not?

We've been laughing together since she was a six-week-old puppy and I took her over to a friend's house for their one-year-old's birthday party. They freaked out thinking I was gifting them and their baby with a puppy. The punchline was I just didn't want to leave her home alone.

Darla was probably giggling as I had to email my sweet neighbor, the one who dropped off a condolence card the other day. I explained that he shouldn't be freaked out if he sees Darla prancing down the street on one of our walks.

She still spends most of the day snoozing behind the couch. I do that thing where I tip toe over to watch, feeling that lump of joy and relief rising up in my throat each time I can see she's breathing.

Your efforts are not wasted, Dear Reader. The calendar tells me this renaissance cannot last forever. I've tucked your email away for the time I will need them.

For now, I'm happy to give Darla this last laugh.

I Leave You With…

25 Things I Learned By 50

So, Brad Pitt, Michelle Obama and I walk into a bar…

Well, not really.

But we could, if we knew each other. There's that.

And we could, if we three were to celebrate something each of us has done in the last 12 months—turn 50 years old.

In honor of my pretend friends' and my mutual milestone, I offer you, Dear Reader, "25 Of The 50 Things I Learned By Time I Turned 50."

Spoiler Alert: If you have yet to turn 50, you might not want to read on, as I wouldn't trade the bumpy, bruising ride it took me to figure these things out on my own. I also wouldn't have believed most of them until 50, some not before 40, and almost none before 30.

Here goes:

1. You will have zits and gray hair at the same time, one of Mother Nature's cruelest jokes. Well, maybe not you, Brad. You've probably never had a pimple in your life.
2. First to marry doesn't necessarily marry best. Would've made those endless weddings in my 20's so much more bearable.
3. Richest, most successful guy in the room will probably also make the worst husband. What you mistake for power, you will discover is a love for himself above all else. (Sorry, Michelle.)
4. Whom someone loves and partners with is no one's business. Doesn't matter their gender, height, or breakfast cereal preference. Just because you don't want to be with someone doesn't mean someone else can't.
5. You can't mess up the right one; Can't make the wrong one work. This is true for all things you try to chase: men, jobs, the perfect house.

6. Weird things don't happen to normal people. There's a reason that "unlucky" friend of yours has drama after drama.
7. I never claimed to be normal.
8. Size does not matter when buying clothes. Buy what fits best.
9. Parents are just people who preceded you on the generational track. Chances are you didn't get a saint, just someone who did their best. Time to own your own issues.
10. Everyone does the best they can all the time. Doesn't mean you have to like it, but accepting it, makes life a whole lot easier and realistic.
11. Most swirling thoughts that make you feel bad include at least one sentence with the word "Should." (He should, she should, I should.)
12. It's time to break up with "Should." Should, says who?
13. Being tired magnifies all emotions. First thing to ask yourself when you fall apart: "How much sleep have I had?"
14. There are few things that can't be made better by either taking a hot shower or walking your dog.
15. No better medicine for a pity party than helping someone else in need. You can't think about your woes while focused on someone else.
16. Biology is over rated. Don't like your crazy relatives? Make your awesome friends your family. Thanksgiving will rock!
17. Biology is over rated, Part Two: Want to be a parent? There are plenty of kids who need parents. Adoption means no stretch marks, well, none you can blame on pregnancy.
18. Your kid won't care about your career success. They care that you're a great mom.
19. Happiness is a choice.
20. The greatest power you will ever have is choosing to be the kind of person you want to be. No one can take your grace, class, or kindness.

21. Throw parties. Lots of parties! Don't wait for your wedding to have your favorite people meet your people.

22. Everything ends. Every job, relationship, and life. We get so excited about beginnings, complacent with middles, and devastated at endings when they are all part of the natural order of things.

23. You will need to reinvent yourself more than once in this life. See #22 for why.

24. "Qi" is an acceptable word when playing "Words With Friends."

25. Stop complaining about your age and getting old. By now, you have at least one friend who has passed who would trade places in a second.

26. So why share only 25 of my 50? Because they only give me so much space and Dear Reader, I would love to know what you could add to the list. What did you learn by 50? Educate me at Daryn@ DarynKagan.com.

Acknowledgements

Thank you, Dear Reader, for this time we've spent together.
Your nodding head when you agree with me.

Not throwing out or deleting this book when I made no sense.

Many thanks to my bosses and editors at Cox Newspapers: Jana Collier, Kevin Riley, Michelle Fong and Bob "Don't Call Me Brian" Underwood, for birthing this columnist.

To Kristin Harmel and John Dedakis, thank you for always being the biggest writing cheerleaders ever.

To my CNN bosses, thank you for not renewing my contract. I'd still be sitting in that anchor seat if you hadn't kicked me out the door. Other big things clearly were waiting.

To My Mr. SummerFest, thank you for all that you are, all that you do, all that you laugh, all those miles you collect.

To my kids, thank you for the daily reminder of how weird I am.

To my friends, my Pretty Ladies, thank you for your love, support, and patience, knowing it takes me awhile to figure this life stuff out.

To DarlaDog, Pisa, and the chickens, thank you for filling that crazy animal lover part of my heart.

About The Author

These days, Daryn's hair is usually up in a scrunchie, but you might remember her more than 12 years as an anchor on CNN when a team of professional make up artists cleaned her up on a regular basis.

She also reported live from several major events around the world, including the war in Iraq, the September 11th terrorist attacks and numerous presidential elections giving her parents plenty to worry about.

Today, Daryn continues her television career as the host of RLTV's "Bookmark," a weekly talk show featuring the top authors of today.

Daryn is also a syndicated newspaper columnist for Cox Newspapers. Her weekly, "What's Possible!" column inspires readers in newspapers across the country.

She is the creator and host of DarynKagan.com, an inspirational online website which features stories fitting the theme, "Show the World What is Possible."

Daryn first book, "What's *Possible! 50 True Stories of People Who Dared To Dream They Could Make a Difference"* can be found online at Amazon.com.

Daryn currently makes her home in Atlanta, Georgia with her husband, daughter, and Little Sister in the Big Brother Big Sister program. There's also one rescue dog, one 3-legged cat, and 9 crazy chickens laying eggs and squawking in her backyard.

All this means more days than not, she reminds herself that she swapped that glamorous TV anchor life to make dinner, drive carpool, and raise two awesome girls.

Oh, and collect fresh eggs.

Thank goodness for fresh eggs.

I'd Love To Come Over

If you enjoyed this book, how about we spend some more time together? I'd love to come speak to your group or corporation. I bring along inspiring stories of people who show the world what's possible.

I also love to speak about reinvention, reinventing your life, your career, your company.

I've also been known to drop in on book clubs around the country. If y'all buy a bunch of my books and I'll Skype to join you for one of your gatherings.

For any of these impossible to resist invitations, you can find me at my website, http://www.DarynKagan.com.

Or drop me a line at Daryn@DarynKagan.com and we'll set it all up.